WHY READ MAIMONIDES TODAY?

Maimonides (Moshe/Moses ben Maimon, 1138–1204) was not only the dominant rabbinic and Jewish intellectual figure of the later medieval period, but also one of history's greatest philosophers. As the author of the *Mishneh Torah* (ca. 1180), a compendium and systematization of the Jewish legal code, he remains an unsurpassed (if not uncontroversial) authority on *halakha* (Jewish law). His philosophical masterpiece, however, is the *Guide of the Perplexed* (1185–1190), in which he systematically presents his views on theology, metaphysics, cosmology, natural science, epistemology, Scriptural hermeneutics, law, and ethics. This accessible and highly readable book introduces the reader to Maimonides' life and thought, and uses a number of enduring and popular philosophical topics – including the problem of evil, freedom of the will, and the relationship between virtue and happiness – to show that he continues to be interesting and relevant to readers today.

STEVEN NADLER is Vilas Research Professor and William H. Hay II Professor of Philosophy at the University of Wisconsin-Madison. His many publications include *Spinoza: A Life* (Cambridge, 1999; second edition, 2018).

WHY READ THEM TODAY?

The books in this series offer new interpretations of thinkers who in different ways reward contemporary re-examination, showing how their thought is particularly relevant to us today.

Books in this Series

STEVEN NADLER, *Why Read Maimonides Today?*

SANDRINE BERGÈS, *Why Read Wollstonecraft Today?*

YUVAL AVNUR, *Why Read Pascal Today?*

WHY READ MAIMONIDES TODAY?

STEVEN NADLER
University of Wisconsin-Madison

CAMBRIDGE
UNIVERSITY PRESS

Shaftesbury Road, Cambridge CB2 8EA, United Kingdom

One Liberty Plaza, 20th Floor, New York, NY 10006, USA

477 Williamstown Road, Port Melbourne, VIC 3207, Australia

314–321, 3rd Floor, Plot 3, Splendor Forum, Jasola District Centre,
New Delhi – 110025, India

103 Penang Road, #05–06/07, Visioncrest Commercial, Singapore 238467

Cambridge University Press is part of Cambridge University Press & Assessment,
a department of the University of Cambridge.

We share the University's mission to contribute to society through the pursuit of
education, learning and research at the highest international levels of excellence.

www.cambridge.org
Information on this title: www.cambridge.org/9781009304788

DOI: 10.1017/9781009304740

© Steven Nadler 2026

This publication is in copyright. Subject to statutory exception and to the provisions
of relevant collective licensing agreements, no reproduction of any part may take
place without the written permission of Cambridge University Press & Assessment.

When citing this work, please include a reference to the DOI 10.1017/9781009304740

First published 2026

A catalogue record for this publication is available from the British Library

A Cataloging-in-Publication data record for this book is available from the Library of Congress

ISBN 978-1-009-30478-8 Hardback
ISBN 978-1-009-30473-3 Paperback

Cambridge University Press & Assessment has no responsibility for the persistence
or accuracy of URLs for external or third-party internet websites referred to in this
publication and does not guarantee that any content on such websites is, or will remain,
accurate or appropriate.

For EU product safety concerns, contact us at Calle de José Abascal, 56, 1°, 28003 Madrid,
Spain, or email eugpsr@cambridge.org

Contents

Acknowledgments	*page* vi
Introduction	1
1 Who Was Maimonides?	11
2 How to Read the Bible	23
3 Why Bad Things Happen to Good People	50
4 Judaism within the Limits of Reason	88
5 Why Read Maimonides Today?	120
References	131
Index	135

Acknowledgments

Several old friends, much more well versed in Maimonides than I, have generously provided their help on this project. I am grateful to Ken Seeskin and Tamar Rudavsky for their feedback on an early draft of the book. And I have profited greatly over the years from conversations with Josef Stern on matters Maimonidean. My thanks especially to Hilary Gaskin for the invitation to take on this challenge in her new series, and to her editorial and production team at Cambridge University Press. My work on this book was supported by funds provided through the William F. Vilas Trust at the University of Wisconsin-Madison, where I am extremely fortunate to be one of the holders of a William F. Vilas Research Professorship.

Introduction

The question "Why read X today?" can legitimately be raised with respect to any premodern thinker, major or minor, in the history of philosophy, and many modern ones as well. Why, one might ask, should we continue to be interested in what philosophers who are so distant from us in time and circumstance had to say? The question is especially acute with respect to those who were writing out of very different concerns and for very different audiences, and whose ideas are uninformed by any philosophical developments (whether new solutions to old questions or new questions altogether) that may have occurred after their time. Indeed, it is not difficult to find contemporary philosophers suggesting that a knowledge of the history of philosophy is irrelevant, and perhaps a genuine hindrance, to doing philosophy – much as scientists might argue that a knowledge of the history of science is irrelevant to doing science – and that perhaps the only reason to learn what earlier thinkers had to say is either to avoid reinventing the wheel or out of purely antiquarian interest.

And yet, has the world and have the circumstances of the human condition really changed so much that there can be no relevance for humanity in the twenty-first century in what Greeks in the fourth century BCE or Arabs in the tenth century or Germans in the eighteenth century thought about human nature and the cosmos? Should we not care about what they had to say on how one can achieve some semblance of happiness, well-being and a good and meaningful life in a world that, then and now, seems to care not at all whether we flourish or founder? Talk about philosophical questions and some of their proffered solutions being "perennial" may be an old chestnut, and we cannot but regard as an exaggeration the remark by the British philosopher Alfred North Whitehead that "the safest generalization about the European philosophical tradition is that it consists of a series of footnotes to Plato."[1] Still, if such aphorisms survive, given the ruthless and not totally unreasonable protest they have long encountered, it must be because they contain some element of truth, even if a bit of work is required to discover it.

The case of Maimonides might seem particularly apt when the question of continued relevance arises. Here we have a twelfth-century rabbi, physician, and civic leader in Muslim Egypt, writing in Judeo-Arabic (Arabic in Hebraic characters) and Hebrew for a very particular audience: medieval Jewish communities throughout the Mediterranean and the Levant, many of whom were suffering persecution in Muslim and Christian lands. Moreover, Maimonides himself tells us that his most important philosophical work, *Guide of the Perplexed*, is not for everyone. There are, he warns us, many truths contained within it that must not be revealed to most people – indeed, that it would be intellectually and spiritually dangerous for them to be exposed to its lessons. There is a hidden wisdom in the *Guide*, and Maimonides would like it to remain hidden for all but a fortunate, well-prepared elite: those who are properly disposed in moral character and in intellect, and, especially important, who are learned both in the Jewish prophetic writings – Torah and the other books of Hebrew Scripture – and in philosophy.

> It is not the purpose of this treatise to make its totality understandable to the vulgar or to beginners in speculation, nor to teach those who have not engaged in any study other than the science of the Law – I mean the legalistic study of the Law. For the purpose of this treatise and of all those like it is the science of the Law in its true sense. Or rather, its purpose is to give indications to a religious man for whom the validity of the Law has become established in his soul and has become actual in his belief – such a man being perfect in his religion and his character, and having studied the sciences of the philosophers and come to know what they signify. (*Guide*, "Introduction to the First Part"; Maimonides 1963: I.5)

Maimonides thus warns us that he has loaded the work with contradictions and falsehoods in order to throw the unprepared reader off the

[1] Whitehead 1979: 39.

scent. "My purpose," he says, "is that the truths be glimpsed and then again be concealed," so that the vulgar, and even those of fine moral character but intellectually underdeveloped, will not be sunk in confusion and lose faith (*Guide*, "Introduction to the First Part"; Maimonides 1963: I.7).[2]

Why, then, should we read today an author who explicitly tells us that most of us should *not* read him?

*

Maimonides (Moshe/Moses ben Maimon, 1138–1204, also known in Jewish tradition as "RaMbaM," the Hebrew acronym for Rabbi Moshe ben Maimon), aside from being the dominant Jewish intellectual figure of the later medieval period, is without doubt – and despite the backlash against his works, which were condemned by some later rabbinic authorities – the greatest of all Jewish philosophers. Appropriately, the famous epitaph on his gravestone reads "from Moses [the prophet] to Moses [Maimonides], there was none like unto Moses."

As the author of the voluminous *Mishneh Torah* (Repetition of the Law, ca. 1180), a compendium and systematization of the Jewish legal code abstracted from the complex debates of the Talmud and other midrashic (rabbinic exegetical) writings, and of a magisterial commentary on the *Mishnah* (the central text of rabbinic law around which the commentaries of the Talmud, called *gemara*, are built) which he composed while still in his twenties, Maimonides is an unsurpassed (if not uncontroversial) authority on *halakha* (Jewish law). His writings have long served as an essential reference in homilies, responsa, and other rabbinic literature, and they continue to be consulted today on legal and ceremonial issues. In the *Guide of the Perplexed*, composed between 1185 and 1190 in Judeo-Arabic and translated into Hebrew in his own lifetime, he systematically laid out his philosophical views on topics in theology, metaphysics, cosmology, natural science, epistemology, Scriptural hermeneutics, law, and ethics.

Why read Maimonides today? First of all, he is one of the greatest, most capacious minds of the High Middle Ages, indeed of all time,

---

[2] This has led several commentators – most famously, Leo Strauss ("How to Begin to Study the Guide of the Perplexed," in Maimonides 1963: I.xi–lvi) – to argue that the *Guide* is subject to both an exoteric and an esoteric reading.

Jewish or otherwise. Here is a philosopher whose works really do (in my estimation) embody deep moral, epistemological, metaphysical, and religious insights that, while ostensibly directed at his fellow Jews, are – and Maimonides himself would agree – of universal import. In this sense, while Maimonides did not reinvent philosophy in the way in which, say, Socrates did, one cannot help but compare the profound wisdom he offers us with that for which Plato's heroic teacher was willing to lay down his life. Maimonides' philosophy – like that of Socrates, the Stoics, the Epicureans, and other ancient thinkers – is intended to be transformative. He wants to direct us on how to change our lives, on how to perfect ourselves through the pursuit of wisdom and achieve the true and highest good for a human being. To the extent that we remain interested in such questions – and well we should – it behooves us to learn what profound thinkers, however distant in the past, have to say about them.

Second, there is the matter of Maimonides' influence. He was a thinker in the Aristotelian tradition, writing in languages inaccessible to most Christians of the time and doing so outside Europe's scholastic philosophical world during the remarkable "renaissance" of the twelfth century and the translation into Latin of much of Aristotle's corpus. Nonetheless, he not only set the agenda for much of subsequent Jewish philosophy but managed to exert some influence on Latin/Christian philosophy as well, especially in the medieval and early modern periods. To be sure, scholars debate how significant Maimonides' impact was beyond the Jewish world. But he was, of all Jewish thinkers, certainly the most read and cited by non-Jewish philosophers. The *Guide* was translated into Latin in the mid-thirteenth century, not long after Maimonides's death. It was, if not very carefully studied, read (at least in part) by such marquee figures as Thomas Aquinas, Albert the Great, Meister Eckart, Nicolas Malebranche, Gottfried Wilhelm Leibniz (who claims to have read the *Guide* and refers to Maimonides as "Rabbi Moses"), and Isaac Newton (who owned a copy of *De Idolatria*, a 1641 Latin translation of Maimonides' *Laws Concerning Idolatry* from the *Mishneh Torah*, as well as four other volumes of the rabbi's writings).[3]

---

[3] On Maimonides in early modern philosophy, see Nadler 2019.

And then there is the case of Bento (Baruch) de Spinoza (1632–1677), the famous "heretic" of Amsterdam, who was deeply influenced, both positively and negatively, by what he read in Maimonides. Because of Spinoza's importance in the history of early modern European philosophy, his remarkable popularity today, and his intimate intellectual relationship to Maimonides, he will play a fairly significant role in several of the chapters of this book. He not only serves as a good example of how a later thinker, far removed in time and culture from twelfth century Egypt, engages with Maimonides, but – given the amount of contemporary interest in Spinoza, and not just among philosophers – he can be seen as part of the brief for why one should read Maimonides today. If you want to understand Spinoza, you have to understand Maimonides.

Third, there is Maimonides's rationalism. Among Anglo-American philosophers, it was long common to construe rationalism as a strictly epistemological position, to be contrasted with empiricism. Rationalists, it was claimed, argued that not all human knowledge derives from experience, and that there was a core of purely rational or *a priori* "ideas" innate in the human mind – true beliefs whose justification did not require any appeal to what the senses might tell us or what experimentation might confirm. Fortunately, we have moved well beyond this narrow understanding of rationalism not only because it is a gross caricature of what the so-called classical rationalists (like Descartes, Spinoza, and Leibniz) actually held but also because rationalism has come to capture a variety of approaches to moral philosophy, philosophy of law, and philosophical theology. Maimonides, especially, offers us a notable example of someone who believed that our *eudaimonia* (an ancient Greek term found in Plato, Aristotle, the Stoics, and the Epicureans, among others, and variously translated as flourishing, well-being, or happiness) is a function of our intellectual achievement. Our true and highest flourishing and happiness is proportionate to the degree to which we have successfully used reason (and not sense experience or the imagination) to understand the cosmos, the natural world around us, and ourselves, as well as to make sense of the laws and moral lessons that, Maimonides believed, were communicated by God to the prophets. For Maimonides and other rationalists, it is the life of reason in which we find our perfection as human beings.

Exhibit A for Maimonides' rationalism is the *Guide of the Perplexed*. For Maimonides' project in that work is nothing less than showing that it is possible to reconcile the articles of faith of the Jewish religion handed down by revelation with demonstrated philosophical or scientific truths discovered through the intellect and rational inquiry. While this might now seem a project of quaint interest, in fact Maimonides's *Guide* is an indispensable text for those who want to see how a major thinker in one religious tradition, eschewing irrational superstition, sought an integration of faith and reason. The "perplexity" with which he was concerned – when religious belief seems, prima facie, to be inconsistent with philosophical or scientific truth – is certainly more than just a mere historical curiosity, as it may, in one form or another, continue to trouble people of faith. The *Guide* also represents the high point of a prominent, if controversial, tradition in Jewish thought of providing a rational justification for all the *mitzvot* or commandments/ laws of the Torah – a project that manifests itself in a variety of religious philosophical traditions as the attempt to model God as a wise and rational being, rather than an arbitrary or "voluntarist" agent who acts by sheer will alone.

Finally, Maimonides can be said to have contributed in an essential way to the transformation of Judaism itself. Much of what we now recognize as "normative" Judaism (which should not be identified merely with what constitutes Orthodox Judaism) – that is, a religion that involves not just the observance of certain rituals and ceremonies and the following of particular legal, ethical, social, and dietary codes but also the acceptance of certain truths or "foundational principles" about God, providential history, and our condition as moral beings – finds its origins in Maimonides' efforts to codify some central doctrines of the Jewish faith. To read Maimonides is to witness a crucial turning point in the history of Judaism, as what one believes becomes as important as what one does.

*

Introductions to Maimonides – broad studies encompassing his halakhic writings (including his responsa as rabbinic authority throughout the Mediterranean world), his medical works, and his grand philosophical treatise – are plentiful. So are focused scholarly studies of particular texts and topics. There is a plethora of outstanding books about the *Guide* itself and its various philosophical dimensions, erudite commentaries on Maimonides' legal and exegetical texts, and quite a few excellent biographies (including four major ones in recent years[4]).

This book falls into none of these categories. It is neither a general introduction to Maimonides nor a scholarly monograph on a particular text or topic. Many of Maimonides' writings – for example, on medical matters – will not be discussed at all. And while the *Guide* will be central to my plan, I will not address all of its major theses. There are, in fact, many reasons to read Maimonides today beyond those I highlight in these chapters. From the perspective of the academic disciplines of Jewish studies (especially the history of Judaism) and religious studies, it is essential to study Maimonides insofar as he represents an important turning point in the development of the Jewish faith. In terms of intellectual history, Maimonides provides a stunning example of how a brilliant polymath of the twelfth century thought about, and influenced others to think about, God, creation, prophecy, immortality, and other topics in rather unorthodox ways. Maimonides has something to offer even to the history of science, as he stands influentially at an important crossroads between Arabic-Muslim and Latin-Christian Aristotelian thinking about the cosmos. Above all, for the great many "lay" (non-academic) readers without any particular disciplinary concerns, especially those with an interest in the nature of Judaism and what it means to be a Jew, they absolutely must read Maimonides, given his substantial contributions to Jewish practice and thought and his continued role as a Torah scholar and legal authority.

As central as all these subjects are for the study of Maimonides, my focus in this book is really on only a small number of themes that, I suggest, any philosophically inclined reader, regardless of his or her religious persuasion or lack thereof, should find sufficiently worth pursuing to go back and read Maimonides' texts themselves. My selection is a highly subjective, even personal, one that reflects my own interests as a philosopher and what I find most intellectually engaging in Maimonides. It represents, as well, why I believe contemporary

---

[4] See the recent biographies by Davidson (2005), Kraemer (2008), Stroumsa (2009), and Halbertal (2014).

readers, especially nonspecialists, should consider reading him. I am certain that other scholars, especially more seasoned Maimonides experts, would both come up with a very different list of topics and fault me for leaving out the ones I do. I am equally certain that some, and perhaps many, will disagree with my interpretations of Maimonides' views. All fair enough. But given the breadth of Maimonides' interests and the volume of his writings, any short book devoted to why we should read Maimonides today will necessarily be highly selective and reflect only the particular interests of the author.

I do not have a religious or reverential bone in my body, and so I cannot recommend turning to Maimonides for insights about how personally to relate to God or how to worship God. And as fascinating as I find Maimonides' attempt to rationalize Jewish law by showing the utility of all of the *mitzvot* of the Torah, my chapter on this part of his project is not meant to inspire observance. Maimonides had a lot to say about a lot of things. But I will focus my discussion on three topics in his writings that, among all the philosophical topics he addresses, might be the most engaging and the most easy and accessible to suggest to readers today.

One theme derives from the objective of the *Guide* itself, namely, perplexity. In particular, it concerns the confusion that may arise when an individual who is either religiously devout or intellectually learned – or, especially, both! – comes upon a passage in the Bible that, from a theological, philosophical or scientific perspective, seems impossible to accept. If the Bible is taken to be a source not just of entertaining and edifying stories but also of truths – about God, the world, human nature, history, or morality – then how is it to be read in such a way that those truths are revealed? What is one to do with biblical texts that, on the face of it, seem false, even absurd? In other words: "How should we read the Bible?" Related to this is what Maimonides regards as the proper conception of God with which any reading of the Bible must be consistent. So a subtheme here, which should be of particular interest to readers of faith, is: "What is God?"

The second theme is an ethical one and concerns the nature of moral luck and the role it may (or may not) play in our lives. It is tempting to think that we are masters of our domains and bear at least some responsibility for how our lives turn out. Despite the obvious deterministic factors that derive from our genetic makeup and the circumstances into which we are born and in which we live, we generally believe that whether our lives turn out to be happy lives well led or lives of misery must depend to some extent on how we exercise our freedom (however one believes "freedom" is to be understood). And yet, ancient thinkers – philosophers, such as Plato and Aristotle, and poets, such as Aeschylus and Sophocles – were only the first to wrestle with the question as to how much an individual's flourishing can be subject to factors beyond their control. For Maimonides, this question arises in the context of his discussion of divine providence and the problem of evil – that is, to put it in more contemporary terms, the philosophical conundrum of why bad things happen to good people (and good things to bad people).

The third theme concerns the nature of Judaism. Religions that are founded on the belief in a supernatural, providential God, as the Abrahamic religions are, are necessarily arational at their core, insofar as the belief in such a being is – depending on your philosophical theologian of choice – above, beyond, or even contrary to reason. There are thinkers, of course, who thought it possible to use reason to prove the existence of God, but an understanding of this deity's innermost essence and modus operandi, and beliefs about much else, are typically regarded as a matter of faith, something that cannot be justified by epistemic (as opposed to moral or psychological) reasons. And yet, Maimonides may go as far as one can go in the Jewish tradition in providing a practical or utilitarian justification of Jewish law, of God's commandments. To this extent – and much to the dismay of some later rabbis – what he offers is a Judaism grounded not in divine power but divine reasonableness. His Judaism is, essentially, a rational religion.

*

In arguing for the continued relevance of Maimonides and why we should still read him, I intend to avoid blatant anachronism. There is no point in trying to show that Maimonides has something to say about democracy, equality, climate change, social justice, or any other issues that dominate the current national, international, and global situation. Perhaps, somewhere in his enormous corpus of writings, one can find solutions to these problems, but it would be a stretch, and it would be unnecessary. We do not need Maimonides to tell us how to resist falling prey to internet conspiracy theories or stop poisoning our planet. Rather, I will focus on those three main topics I have highlighted as central to Maimonides' philosophical program.

In New York City in the 1960s, there was a ubiquitous advertising campaign for a brand of rye bread that bore the tag line: "You don't have to be Jewish to love Levy's real Jewish rye." Posters in subway stations, the sides of buses, and in newspaper and magazines ads showed people of all ethnicities – Blacks, East Asians, South Asians, Indigenous Americans, as well as Hasidic Jews – enjoying sandwiches made on Levy's bread.

My campaign for why we should read Maimonides today might be taken in a similar vein. Maimonides is not for Jewish readers alone. This is certainly not news to people who have studied the *Guide*, which covers philosophical topics that transcend any particular religious tradition. Maimonides did initially write the work in a language that would be accessible primarily to Jews – in fact, primarily to certain Jews, namely, those capable of reading Judeo-Arabic. But he was no doubt aware of the universal import of what he had to say. So were his earliest translators and their gentile readers. Just two decades or so after Maimonides' death, Christian scholars were familiar with the content of the *Guide* through partial Latin translations; by the 1240s, they were studying a complete Latin translation. Any reader of the *Guide* today cannot fail to regard it not only as an important work of Jewish philosophy but as a vitally interesting work of philosophy, period.

Now I would take all this one step further: you do not have to believe in God or be a person of any religious faith whatsoever in order to glean important philosophical insights and derive some very fine wisdom from this very Jewish but (in the eyes of his contemporary and later critics) very unorthodox thinker. I do hope to encourage readers of faith to turn to Maimonides, especially if they find themselves plagued by the kind of "perplexity" he wants to alleviate. But even secular readers, whether they are atheists or agnostics, should find reading Maimonides a profoundly fascinating, moving and enlightening experience. I hope with this short book to provide a few reasons why.

CHAPTER I

Who Was Maimonides?

From Andalusia to Fez to Fustat

Maimonides was born in Córdoba, in Andalusia, in 1137 or 1138. His father, Maimon, was a *dayyan* or Jewish court judge, and thus held a high position in the flourishing Córdoba Jewish community. The family seems to have been sufficiently well-off, perhaps through the kind of mercantile activities in which many Iberian Jews engaged.

Under earlier Umayyad Muslim rule of *Al-Andalus*, the beginning of a period known as *La Convivencia*, Jews enjoyed what has often been regarded as a kind of "Golden Age." They benefited from a relatively high degree of toleration and economic success and served the Muslim caliphate in a variety of capacities: as courtiers, physicians, financial advisers, intellectuals, even military leaders. While the transition to stricter Almoravid rule at the end of the eleventh century led to substantial and not always welcome changes for Jewish communities, life in Córdoba remained stable enough for most families to want to stay put.

Things took a serious turn for the worse, however, in 1147, with the Almohad invasion from Berber North Africa. The new, fundamentalist, and far less tolerant rulers sought, through forced conversions, to impose Islam throughout their realm. Many Jews and Christians fled Andalusia, either for non-Muslim Iberian territory – Toledo was now under Christian control – or further east, to Provence. While Maimonides' family left Córdoba, they remained within Andalusia, at least for a while. At some point, however – perhaps around 1160 – and somewhat curiously, they landed in Fez, Morocco, the religious and administrative center of the Almohad domain. Out of the pot and into the fire, so to speak. Scholars have long debated whether or not Maimon and his family converted to Islam, either in Andalusia or Fez; the fact that the clan remained within the Almohad realm is often taken as evidence in favor of their conversion.[1] There can be little doubt, however, that, if they did indeed convert, they continued to observe Judaism in secret.

In his "Epistle on Apostasy," Maimonides discourages martyrdom and condones conversion (at least in words) when forced under threat of violence, although he also counsels eventual emigration to safer lands where one can return openly to Judaism. When faced with the choice between uttering the words of the Muslim confession and death, Maimonides says that

> Verily, one who has preferred to suffer martyrdom in order not to pronounce the Mohammedan confession, has done nobly and well and his reward is great before the Lord. He may be regarded as supremely virtuous as he was willing to surrender his life for the sanctification of the name of God. Should one, however, inquire of me: "Shall I be slain or pronounce the Mohammedan confession?", my answer would be "Utter the formula and live." To be sure, one should not continue to live in such an environment, but until the opportunity presents itself to leave one should be confined to the privacy of his home and conduct his transactions in secret. For this kind of apostasy directed exclusively at compelling verbal confession is unique. Our rabbis' contention of "better to suffer death than to commit a transgression" was never meant to imply a single transgression without action.[2]

Whether or not Maimonides and his family did pay lip service to the Muslim faith, they eventually opted for emigration. In 1165, Maimonides, along with his father and two brothers – we do not know anything about his mother – departed for the Holy Land, where they lived for a time in Acre. Within the year, however, they were in Egypt (in violation of the ancient rabbinic prohibition against dwelling in the land of the pharaohs). Maimonides settled first in Alexandria, a center of Mediterranean commerce with a large Jewish population, and then in cosmopolitan Fustat, part of greater Cairo and home to

---

[1] Davidson (2005), Kraemer (2008) and Stroumsa (2009) do not all agree on this point.
[2] Translation from Stitskin 1973: 107.

three synagogues. He would remain there until his death in 1204. It was during this transitional period, moving from Fez, where he continued the medical education he had begun in Andalusia, to Palestine to Egypt, that Maimonides, remarkably, began composing his first major work, the *Commentary on the Mishnah*. In this magisterial treatise, written in Judeo-Arabic, the twenty-three-year-old Maimonides first presents his "Thirteen Articles of the Jewish Faith." As they appear in the commentary on Sanhedrin, Chapter 10 ("All of Israel has a place [*helek*] in the world to come [*olam ha-ba*]"), these are, in summary form:

1. That there is one God, the creator of all things.
2. That God is one.
3. That God the creator has no body and there can be no comparison between God and matter.
4. That God is eternal.
5. That God alone is to be worshipped; to God alone is it permissible to pray.
6. That there are genuine prophets whose words are true and to be heeded.
7. That Moses was the greatest of all prophets.
8. That the Torah as we have it was given to Moses by God.
9. That the Torah was correctly and incorrigibly transmitted from God, and may suffer no alteration.
10. That God the creator knows all the deeds and thoughts of human beings.
11. That God rewards those who follow the commandments of the Torah and punishes those who transgress them.
12. That the Messiah will come.
13. That there will be a resurrection of the dead and they shall be returned to life when it pleases God to do so.

These thirteen principles represent the first time that an authoritative Jewish intellectual figure attempted to lay out, in such dogmatic fashion, a creed or essential tenets of Judaism. Belief, on Maimonides' account, was just as important as ritual observance.[3]

---

[3] On this, see Kellner 2004. Maimonides' attempt at dogmatism had very mixed results and was rejected by many.

Saladin's Physician, Fustat's Rabbi

Maimonides experienced Egypt under both the relatively liberal Fatimids and then the more austere Ayyubids. The Ayyubid sultan, Saladin, an ambitious leader who sought to extend his power throughout the Mediterranean and the Levant, recognized Maimonides' skills as a doctor and as a teacher of the sciences. Through his vizier (high minister) al-Qadi al-Fadil, he thus appointed him as one of his court physicians, although it is unclear from the sources whether Maimonides actually treated Saladin himself. The sultan and his vizier also saw that Maimonides' learning and personal charisma, as well as the respect accorded him by his fellow Jews, made him the natural leader of "his people." Thus, in 1171 they appointed Maimonides "Head of the Jews" (*ra'is al yahud*) in Egypt. This position entailed managing religious, political, legal, social, and business issues within the community, as well as serving as the Jewish representative before the Muslim regime. Although Maimonides occupied this official position for only two years, his religious and moral authority was so great that he was, in effect, "the Great Rav" until the end of his life.

It was in Egypt that Maimonides composed his two greatest works of theology, religious law, and philosophy. In the 1170s, he wrote the multivolume legal treatise *Mishneh Torah* (in Hebrew), in which he summarily and systematically – on the basis of some preliminary philosophical and theological foundations – covers all of Jewish law, ceremony, and observance. What is most notable (and, for his Jewish readers, useful) about the work is the way in which Maimonides selectively stipulates the law by leaving out the argumentative back and forth between the different "houses" or rabbinic authorities that makes it such a challenge to distill unambiguous, authoritative rulings from the Talmud itself.

Mishneh Torah

There is a good deal of metaphysics, epistemology, physics, and moral philosophy in the *Mishneh Torah*, especially the first book, the *Sefer ha-Maddah* (The Book of Knowledge), and its opening section, *Hilkhot Yesodai ha-Torah* (Laws of the Foundations of the Torah). In these chapters Maimonides treats the existence of God, the process of divine creation, the structure of the cosmos (with its crystalline heavenly spheres and the celestial bodies embedded in them), the "fundamental elements" of the terrestrial realm, and the nature of the human being as a union of body and soul. Much of this material is presented in good Aristotelian terms. The four elements that, in their various mixtures, constitute "all the creations below the sky" and account for the characteristic behaviors of inanimate things are earth, air, fire, and water. Natural substances are introduced as hylomorphic creatures composed of basic matter and an animating immaterial form (with the human soul serving as the substantial form of the human body). The philosophical opening texts of the *Mishneh Torah* also review some detailed matters of Jewish law (the *mitzvot*), including various species of transgression and their punishment, and offers an extended analysis of the nature of prophecy and the prophet's role in society.

Guide of the Perplexed

Maimonides' most important philosophical work – and arguably his most famous text – is the *Guide of the Perplexed*, which he wrote, in Judeo-Arabic, between 1185 and 1190. The *Guide* is a monumental work of philosophical theology, metaphysics, cosmology, natural science, ethics, legal philosophy, epistemology, and biblical textual exegesis. The intellectual influences on the *Guide* are many and diverse. Aside from his Jewish sources – the philosophers include Judah Halevi and Saadya ben Joseph – there is Plato; Aristotle and his commentators (especially Alexander of Aphrodisias); Arabic philosophers such as al-Farabi, ibn Sina (Avicenna), and ibn Rushd (Averroës); and the Muslim theologians known as the Mutakallimun, both the doctrinaire Asharites (e.g., al-Ghazali) and the more rationalist Mutazilite school.[4]

Many of Maimonides' working hours were taken up by composing *responsa*, letters in which he replies to queries from other rabbis or scholars, perhaps offering guidance on a matter of *halakha* (Jewish law), or addresses some religious, social, or political matter arising in

---

[4] On Maimonides' sources in the *Guide*, see Pines' introduction in Maimonides 1963: lvii–cxxxiv, and Ivry 2005.

one Jewish community or another. His "Epistle to Yemen," for example, which he composed in the early 1170s, was Maimonides' response to the head of the Yemenite Jewish community who had written to him about their persecution by local Shi'ite Muslims. Maimonides encouraged the rabbi and his people to remain strong in their faith and saw in their suffering a prelude to the coming of the Messiah.

The *Guide of the Perplexed* can itself be regarded as a kind of *responsum*, albeit a rather extended one. It takes the literary form of a letter to his former student Joseph ben Judah. Joseph, who was now living in Aleppo, had written to Maimonides seeking intellectual counsel. The problem, as Maimonides describes it, is that Joseph is suffering from a kind of "perplexity." He notes that Joseph is an instance of "a religious man for whom the validity of our Law has become established in his soul and has become actual in his belief – a man perfect in his religion and his character." He is expert in "the science of the Law," that is, the legalistic study of Torah and rabbinic halakhic commentary. He has also studied, under Maimonides' tutelage, mathematics, astronomy, and logic, as well as "the sciences of the philosophers." This has awakened in him not only a great desire to learn the deeper secrets of the prophetic books, of which Maimonides has given him "certain flashes" and "certain indications," but to understand "the science of the Law in its true sense," that is, "the divine science," the fundamental truths on "divine matters" on which the Law rests – what Maimonides calls "the foundations of the Law" (*Guide*, Introduction to the First Part; Maimonides 1963: I.5).

Perplexity

The problem, Maimonides notes, is that what one might learn from the philosophers could appear to be inconsistent with what one finds in Scripture, at least when it is read in a literal or superficial way.

> The human intellect having drawn him on and led him to dwell within its province, he must have felt distressed by the externals of the Law and by the meanings of the above-mentioned equivocal, derivative, or amphibolous terms, as he continued to understand them by himself or was made to understand them by others. Hence he would remain in

a state of perplexity and confusion as to whether he should follow his intellect, renounce what he knew concerning the terms in question, and consequently consider that he has renounced the foundations of the Law. Or he should hold fast to his understanding of these terms and not let himself be drawn on together with his intellect, rather turning his back on it and moving away from it, while at the same time perceiving that he had brought loss to himself and harm to his religion. He would be left with those imaginary beliefs to which he owes his fear and difficulty and would not cease to suffer from heartache and great perplexity. (*Guide*, Introduction to the First Part; Maimonides 1963: I.5–6)

On one level, the perplexity seems rather straightforward: it appears to be a matter of a difficulty in reconciling religious beliefs, as derived from a canonical text or tradition, with rational philosophical and scientific truths. What is one to do when things taken on faith and authority appear to clash with things known through reason or sense experience?

Consider, for example, a person who is born into a fundamentalist religious family. Her whole upbringing and education are based solely on the Bible and other religious texts. She is not exposed to any secular studies whatsoever: no science, no philosophy, no history, no literature. Her faith is firm and an essential part of her identity. She believes that God created the world in six days, that human beings and other species were produced by special and distinct acts of creation, that the earth is less than ten thousand years old, and so on. Then, one day, she is exposed to some scientific literature. Perhaps she goes off to university and learns about a Big Bang occurring 13.8 billion years ago. She reads that human beings and other species evolved through random variations and a process of natural selection. She still believes in God, but begins to wonder whether God can be like the personal, anthropomorphic agent depicted in the Bible. Can there really be, in a causally deterministic universe governed by laws of nature, miracles, that is, divinely caused suspensions or violations of those laws? She is convinced that there is something to all of the new theories; they are backed up by sophisticated theorizing and experimental results, and so must in some sense be accepted. But she does not know how to square what she knows to be scientifically or philosophically true with everything she has believed since childhood. She cannot abandon her faith, but neither can she dismiss the science and philosophy. She is, in short, perplexed.

To put the problem in this superficial way, however, is somewhat misleading. For one thing, it is not just a matter of a literal reading of the words of the Bible being irreconcilable with what science and philosophy have demonstrated – "where external sense manifestly contradicts the truth and departs from the intelligible," as Maimonides puts it. Joseph also wants to understand the parables of Scripture, which are opaque and difficult to interpret. There is a more profound meaning to these narratives to be discovered. Maimonides insists, for example, that the creation story of the Bible, "the Account of the Beginning [*Ma'aseh Bereshit*]" is, in fact, natural science, which Scripture conveys "in very obscure words." Joseph would like the obscurity lifted and the secrets revealed.

Moreover, Joseph, the paradigm of perplexity, is not a man of simple faith who is now confronting a new and foreign body of knowledge that contradicts that faith. He is a scholar, an erudite reader of Torah and other Jewish texts and learned in Jewish law. And yet, the legal learning he has acquired is not enough. He wants to deepen his understanding of the law. As Maimonides describes him, he is endowed with a "strong desire for inquiry and ... a powerful longing for speculative matters" (*Guide*, Epistle Dedicatory; Maimonides 1963: I.3). Joseph's studies in astronomy and other "philosophical" subjects are not pursued for their own sake but in order to give him a more profound insight into God, the author of the Law; the cosmos God has created; and what this all means for human beings.

The problem, however, is that different sources are leading him in different ways. The prophetic books of Judaism and works of Kalam theology do not seem to be entirely coherent among themselves, much less with truths that are philosophically sound. Neither are all the philosophers in agreement; Plato says one thing and Aristotle another, while Aristotle's commentators do not all read him the same way.

Part of Joseph's trouble, and one of the reasons for his perplexity, is that he is going about his pursuit of understanding in the wrong way. His unsystematic and haphazard approach is only compounding his confusion. "His longing is stronger than his grasp," Maimonides says. "I did not cease ... enjoining upon you to approach matters in an orderly manner." His purpose in composing the *Guide*, then, was that "the truth should be established in your mind according to the proper methods and that certainty should not come to you by accident" (*Guide*, Epistle Dedicatory; Maimonides 1963: I.3–4).

The perplexity with which Maimonides is concerned in the *Guide*, then, is a rare and profound phenomenon. A devoutly religious person who does not just *live* by the law – Jewish law – but has closely *studied* the law, Torah, and knows it well wants also to *understand* the law and learn its "secrets," its foundations, and its rationale. If, as Maimonides says, the creation story of *Bereshit* (Genesis) is natural science, he wants to see how this is so. If the writings of the prophets can be read in a way consistent with what philosophy demonstrates as true, then he wants the key. And if the narratives of the Bible bear theological and metaphysical truths not evident on the surface, he wants to know how to discover them.

As Maimonides goes about resolving Joseph's perplexity (as well as that of any sufficiently prepared reader), he also undertakes to dispel a number of superstitious beliefs. In fact, this is an essential step in the way out of perplexity. Among such beliefs to be corrected are those about God, including any anthropomorphizing that depicts God in bodily terms; about the working of divine providence, which cannot involve some personal deity handing out rewards and punishments but rather must be simply the natural protection that understanding brings in the face of nature's vicissitudes; about what awaits us in the world-to-come; and about the relationship between virtue and happiness or well-being.

The perplexity, then, is not merely an epistemological problem, not just a case of cognitive dissonance. It is deeper than that, more personal, more practical, even existential. For the ultimate philosophical secrets of the prophets concern how we are to live. Here lies the gist of the *Guide* – indeed, the central concern of all of Maimonides' major writings, even his halakhic works. What Joseph is in need of is a kind of therapy. He needs correction, to be put on the right path of living and of thinking. He needs to know what constitutes a good life for a human being and how to achieve it. In the *Guide*, Maimonides points out that the way to attaining the true human good is through a life of reason and knowledge, a life under the guidance of the intellect.

If the *Mishneh Torah* represents a systematizing of Jewish law, the *Guide* represents the rationalizing or "philosophizing" of Jewish faith –

something that did not sit well with his later rabbinic critics, who within a century would instigate the book's burning because they saw it as reducing that faith to a mere handmaiden of philosophy.

Father, Brother, Rabbi, Physician

We actually know very little about the details of Maimonides' personal life. He did marry relatively late in life, when he was in his thirties, although it is unclear whether this was his first or second marriage. His wife was the daughter of a government official, a secretary to Saladin's wife, but we do not know her name. He had a son, Abraham, and may also have had a daughter who died as a child.

And then there was Maimonides' beloved younger brother, David. The two men were extremely close, both personally and professionally. They were engaged together in the trade of precious stones and other rich commodities, perhaps following in their father's mercantile footsteps. But tragedy struck when David, who was on a business trip to India, died in a shipwreck. Maimonides was inconsolable. It is worth quoting at length from a letter to a judge in Acre in which Maimonides relates the deep and debilitating sadness he felt over this loss.

> A few months after we departed from [the Land of Israel], my father and master died (may the memory of the righteous be a blessing). Letters of condolences arrived from the furthest west and from the land of Edom ... yet you disregarded this. Furthermore, I suffered many well-known calamities in Egypt, including sickness, financial loss and the attempt by informers to have me killed. The worst disaster that struck me of late, worse than anything I had ever experienced from the time I was born until this day, was the demise of that upright man (may the memory of the righteous be a blessing), who drowned in the Indian Ocean while in possession of much money belonging to me, to him and to others, leaving a young daughter and his widow in my care. For about a year from the day the evil tidings reached me I remained prostrate in bed with a severe inflammation, fever and mental confusion, and well nigh perished. From then until this day, that is about eight years, I have been in a state of disconsolate mourning. How can I be consoled? For he was my son; he grew up upon my knees; he was my brother, my pupil. It was he who did business in the marketplace, earning a livelihood, while I dwelled in security. He had a ready grasp of Talmud and a superb

mastery of grammar. My only joy was to see him. "The sun has set on all joy." [Isa. 24:11.] For he has gone on to eternal life, leaving me dismayed in a foreign land. Whenever I see his handwriting or one of his books my heart is churned inside me and my sorrow is rekindled ... And were it not for the Torah, which is my delight, and for scientific matters, which let me forget my sorrow, "I would have perished in my affliction" [Ps. 119:92].[5]

Despite the years of mourning and, it seems, depression, Maimonides had to carry on. There were teaching, judicial, medical, and rabbinic duties to attend to, and not just for the Fustat and Cairo communities. Maimonides was, in effect, through his letters and responsa, the communicating rabbi for congregations across the Levant.

While Maimonides was utterly devoted to his broad rabbinic and communal role, he rued the amount of time it required. Writing in 1191 to his former student Joseph, he complains about how little time he has for his true love, study and scholarship, given the incessant demands of his day job:

> I tell you that I have become known as a physician among the mighty, such as the chief judge, the emirs, and the house of al-Fadil and the other princes of the land, those who lack nothing. But as for the masses, I am beyond their reach, and they have no way to approach me. And this causes me to spend the entire day in Cairo, tending to the sick, and when I get back to Fustat, all I can do for the rest of the day and into the night is to examine the medical texts that I need to consult ... As a result, I do not have a moment to study Torah except on the Sabbath, and as for other sciences, I do not have a moment to study any of them, and this harms me greatly.[6]

It is fascinating to compare Maimonides' complaint here with that lodged by an equally monumental thinker from another religious tradition many centuries earlier. Saint Augustine (354–430) wanted nothing more than to get back to work on his philosophical/theological magnum opus, the *City of God*. Writing also in a letter, he bemoans the time away from that intellectual project required by his duties as bishop of Hippo, especially the sermons he owes to various Christian congregations and

---

[5] Translation from Kraemer 2008: 255–6.   [6] Quoted in Halbertal 2014: 63–64.

the responses he must make to random requests for his opinion on this or that matter.

> I am annoyed because of the demands that are thrust upon me to write, arriving unannounced, from here, there, and everywhere. They interrupt and hold up all the other things that we have so neatly lined up in order. They never seem to stop.[7]

We see Maimonides in his letter to Joseph likewise struggling to balance a devotion to his time-consuming obligations as a rabbi and physician, especially to healing the sick among the wealthy and the poor, with his personal desire for the opportunity to engage in the study of Torah and other religious and philosophical texts. It was a tension that would plague him for the rest of his life, especially in the 1190s, when once again he was named Head of the Jews in Egypt.

The constant cares and burdens of his various roles no doubt took a toll on Maimonides' health, which was apparently never very robust. He complains in his letters over the years about various infirmities and the little time he had to rest and get better. With the new increase in his duties as communal head, it was all too much for a man in his sixties. Ill and exhausted, he died in 1204.

---

[7] Augustine 1989: 168–9.

CHAPTER 2

How to Read the Bible

Readers coming to the *Guide of the Perplexed* for the first time may find themselves perplexed by the work's opening sections. Perhaps expecting some profound pearls of wisdom about God, the world or human nature, what they discover instead is a long series of entries – over three-dozen chapters – on Hebrew semantics and etymology, along with exegeses of passages from the Hebrew Bible (also called *TaNaKh*, the Hebrew acronym for the Pentateuch/*Torah*, the texts of the prophets/ *Nevi'im*, and other writings/*Ketuvim*). Chapters are devoted to the ambiguity of such mundane words as "foot," "eye," "standing" and "sitting," "rock," and "touch." Maimonides explains how the Hebrew word for "eat" can refer both to the taking in of food by living beings and to any kind of destruction or undoing, and that "face" can signify either the familiar front part of the head or emotional states like "anger and wrath" (as in "He set his face against them").

The *Guide* thereby starts out with a long disquisition on the multiple meanings of terms found throughout the Bible, especially those terms that ordinarily describe bodies and the actions of living things but that also are used to refer to the Abrahamic God and his modus operandi. It looks more like a lexicon than a treatise of philosophy. In fact, these opening chapters deal with one of Maimonides' most important philosophical and theological theses: the incorporeality of God. There are many things we might rightly or wrongly, and more or less harmlessly, imagine about God, but there is at least one thing that we must absolutely *never* believe, namely, that God has a body.

Whatever God is – and for Maimonides there is very little that can be said essentially and positively about God, whose reality transcends both our categories of thinking and the limits of language – God is not a physical being. Despite the very human ways in which the Bible describes God, God does not have a face, hands, or feet. God does not sit or stand or walk. God does not literally speak or listen. And if there is a sense in which God is "visible," it is not because God can actually be seen.

> Our whole purpose [in this chapter] was to show that whenever the words *seeing*, *vision*, and *looking* occur [in the Bible] in this sense, intellectual apprehension is meant, and not the eye's sight, as God, may He be exalted, is not an existent that can be apprehended with the eyes. (*Guide* I.5; Maimonides 1963: I.31)

Human beings may have been created "in the likeness of God." But this should not be taken to mean that God looks and acts like we do. This corporeal conception of God was common among people who, reading the biblical texts, took God's declaration "Let us make man in our image" to mean "that God was a body provided with a face and a hand, like them in shape and configuration" (*Guide* I.1; Maimonides 1963: I.21). But any such bodily representation of God is irreconcilable with God's infiniteness, eternity, uniqueness, unity, immutability, and absolute simplicity, all of which imply a purely spiritual being. There is no respect whatsoever in which God is like us, or like any bodily being. There are false beliefs about God that are not particularly, or at least not obviously, prejudicial to faith and to the proper conception of the deity – for example, that God is subject to such psychological states as jealousy and anger; or that God, in some sense (if not verbally), issues commands or actively exercises providence. In fact, these things, as we shall see, are not truly predicable of God, and strictly speaking they are difficult to reconcile with what is supposed to be God's total lack of change and plurality. But perhaps for those of simple faith, especially among the masses, they may be relatively harmless beliefs. However, the idea that God has a body not only is inconsistent with indubitably certain philosophical truths about God but undermines any true worship, not least because it encourages, and is even a form of, idolatry. This is something that Maimonides emphasizes not only in the *Guide*, intended as it is for an elite audience, but also in his Hebrew halakhic writings, including the *Mishneh Torah*.

> Since it has been clarified that He does not have a body or corporeal form, it is also clear that none of the functions of the body are appropriate to Him: neither connection nor separation, neither place nor measure, neither ascent nor descent, neither right nor left, neither front nor back, neither standing nor sitting. (*Mishneh Torah*, Hilkhot Yesodei Ha-Torah, I.11)

All of the corporeal characterizations of God in the Bible are due to the fact that, as Maimonides reminds us many times, the prophetic writings "speak in the language of man." The ancient, divinely inspired authors of these texts accommodated their words to the naïveté and understanding of the multitude.

> Hence, attributes indicating corporeality have been predicated of Him in order to indicate that He, may He be exalted, exists, inasmuch as the many cannot at first conceive of any existence save that of a body alone; thus, that which is neither a body nor existent in a body does not exist in their opinion. (*Guide* I.26; Maimonides 1963: I.56)

The Bible's materialist *façons de parler* are designed to take advantage of ordinary people's prejudices and prompt them to acknowledge God's *existence*, but no one should take them to be revealing something about God's nature and be misled into thinking that God literally has a body. People of learning, of course – and this includes philosophers and the prophets themselves – know better. With an informed understanding of God, they can approach passages that give bodily form to God in the right hermeneutical frame of mind. They know, that is, how to read the Bible.

Biblical Literalism

There are certainly many devout readers of the Bible today who interpret it literally – nearly a third of Americans, according to one poll. For fundamentalist and evangelical Christians, absolutely every word is to be taken in its plainest sense, and every sentence explicitly conveys a truth. Such biblical literalists, believing as they do that the Bible is the actual word of God, insist that it would be sacrilegious to depart from what seems to be its most obvious intended meanings. There is still room for interpretation. Even the literal meaning of a sentence may not be especially obvious; or there may be apparent inconsistencies between different sentences, each of which seems, by itself, to be perfectly clear. In such cases, some background or contextual information on language or history might be required to make (literal) sense of things. But for the literalist, none of this means one ought to ever opt for a figurative or metaphorical reading. Thus, the days of divine creation proceeded exactly as described in Genesis. Miracles abound in the Bible – seas part, heavenly bodies stand still – with the order of nature often disrupted for some providential end. Angelic beings wrestle with humans, and at one time people lived for centuries. To the literalist, all of this is genuinely true.

The doctrine of biblical literalism was well formulated at a conference of Christian evangelical leaders organized in 1982 by the International Council on Biblical Inerrancy:

> We affirm the necessity of interpreting the Bible according to its literal, or normal, sense. The literal sense is the grammatical-historical sense, that is, the meaning of which the writer expressed. Interpretation according to the literal sense will take account of all figures of speech and literary forms found in the text.
>
> We deny the legitimacy of any approach to Scripture that attributes to it meaning which the literal sense does not support.[1]

There are, obviously, many complications with this view, not the least being the potential for disagreement as to what any word or sentence *literally* means, especially in context. What counts as a "literal reading" depends on what one takes the basic meaning of a word or a phrase to be. "He's a pain in the neck" could refer to the fact that another person is pressing on my upper spine; or, it could be argued, it refers in colloquial English in an equally literal way to the fact that he is causing me a lot of trouble.

Maimonides' concern with literalism, however, is fairly straightforward. The Bible, he insists, must be read in such a way that it satisfies two conditions: first, it must not contravene any demonstrated truth; second, it must not undermine any of the basic principles of

---

[1] The Chicago Statement on Biblical Hermeneutics, Article XV, https://defendinginerrancy.com/chicago-statements.

faith. And from both of these conditions it follows that the Bible must never, ever be read to imply that God is a corporeal being.

Equivocal Words

Consider the following biblical passages: "And the figure of the Lord shall he look upon" (Numbers 12:8); "And God saw that it was good" (Genesis 1:3); "Blessed be the glory of the Lord in his place" (Ezekiel 3:12); "Thus said the Lord, the heaven is my throne" (Isaiah 66:1); "God who sits in heaven" (Psalm 123:1); "And God's feet shall stand on that day on the Mount of Olives" (Zechariah 14:4); and "God sorrowed unto His heart" (Genesis 6:6).

The God portrayed in these and other texts is a very anthropomorphic deity. This God has a visible (human) shape and exists in localized places. He "walks" (with his feet?) through the Garden of Eden, where he "sees" (with his eyes?) the human beings he has created. He "speaks" (with his mouth?) to Adam and Eve, to Moses, to Job. He sits on a "throne" in the heavens, but occasionally comes down to wander the earth. Moreover, the biblical God's psyche runs through a gamut of mental states. God has beliefs, volitions, and emotions. God wants to know where Adam and Eve are in the Garden of Eden ("Where are you?", he wonders in Genesis 3:9). God reminds the Israelites that "The Lord your God is a jealous God" (Deuteronomy 4:24). The prophet Ezekiel conveys God's warning that "I will soon pour out my wrath upon you and spend my anger against you" (Ezekiel 7:8). God is pleased, angry, jealous, vengeful, even ignorant, and suspicious. At least, this is what these and many other passages say if they are read literally, with the ordinary and straightforward understanding of such terms as "feet," "heart," "sit," "throne," "sorrow," "wrath," and so on.

However, all of these terms, and many others, Maimonides says, are "equivocal." They have multiple meanings, and signify different things in different contexts. A good example of an equivocal term is the word "mean" in the following two sentences: "He is a mean person" and "That was a mean storm." In the cases with which Maimonides is concerned, the aforementioned words mean one thing when they are applied to creatures such as us and another thing entirely when they are used with respect to God. When they are used to refer to natural agents and their actions, they typically have their ordinary meaning. Human beings have eyes to see and feet with which to walk; they can sit on a throne or rise up from it; and they have feelings of sorrow and joy – all these ascriptions are to be understood literally. On the other hand, when the terms are used to describe God's being or actions, they cannot be taken in their literal sense. As Maimonides explains with respect to eyes and vision,

> Know that the three words *to see, to look at*, and *to vision* are applied to the sight of the eye and that all three of them are also used figuratively to denote the grasp of the intellect. As for the verb *to see*, this is generally admitted by the multitude. Thus it says: "And he saw, and behold a well in the field" [Exodus 25:9]. This refers to the sight of the eye. But it also says: "Yea, my heart hath seen much of wisdom and knowledge" [Exodus 25:40]; and this refers to intellectual apprehension. Every mention of seeing, when referring to God, may He be exalted, has this figurative meaning. As when Scripture says "I saw the Lord"; "And the Lord became seen to him"; "And God saw that it was Good". All this refers to intellectual apprehension and in no way to the eye's seeing, as the eye can only apprehend a body, one that is placed in some direction and, in addition, with some of the accidents of the body. (*Guide* I.4; Maimonides 1963: I.28)

God, as an absolutely simple being devoid of parts and multiplicity, does not (cannot) have a body, insofar as bodies are necessarily complex and made up of divisible parts. Therefore, God does not have eyes and cannot literally see; nor, lacking bodily form, can God literally be seen. In such cases, then, the sentences employing corporeal language must be given a figurative or metaphorical reading. "Seeing," when used for God, means understanding; "standing" means enduring; "sitting" means presiding over or ruling; "touching" means drawing near cognitively, through thinking about something; and "foot" refers to cause or foundation. God might not literally walk through the Garden of Eden, but God is present there in His own unique way.

Anthropomorphizing God

It is not only the corporeal representation of God that troubles Maimonides and motivates the case for the figurative reading of certain biblical texts. He is opposed to any kind of anthropomorphization or personalization of God whatsoever. This includes taking literally descriptions of God in psychological and moral terms drawn from the ways in which human beings think and act.

It is common to conceive of the Abrahamic God as knowledgeable and willful, and the Bible seems to encourage us to do so. God is not only a passionate and emotional deity, as we have seen, but is endowed with cognitive states as well. He has beliefs and expectations and makes judgments; God wants his commands to be followed and threatens disobedience with punishment. This God is also good, wise, just, and merciful. God, in other words, appears in the Bible as a kind of person, a moral agent very much like ourselves. However, Maimonides insists, these attributions to God of human-like mental states and character traits should no more be taken literally and at face value than the corporeal descriptions of God. Just as one must accept that "God is not a body," so it must be granted that

> there is absolutely no likeness in any respect whatever between Him and the things created by Him; that His existence has no likeness to theirs; nor His life to the life of those among them who are live; nor again His knowledge to the knowledge of those among them who are endowed with knowledge. [People] should be made to accept the belief that the difference between Him and them is not merely a difference of more and less, but one concerning the species of existence. (*Guide* I.35; Maimonides 1963: I.80)

The Bible mentions God's "seeing," but because God does not have eyes we must read this figuratively as a reference to God's knowledge and understanding. And yet it is clear, as well, that even such epistemic acts as knowing and understanding must be said of God in only a figurative or metaphorical way, since there is no resemblance whatsoever between how God "knows" and how we know. We have no access whatsoever to what it must be like for God to know. (There is a famous article about mind and consciousness by the philosopher Thomas Nagel titled "What Is It Like to Be a Bat?,"[2] in which, as he argues for the ineffability and irreducibility of consciousness, he points out that we cannot possibly understand how a bat, working through echolocation, consciously

---

[2] Nagel 1974.

experiences the world. In Maimonidean terms, the article could just as well have been titled "What Is It Like to Be God?") The doctrine of equivocity holds across the board, to body *and* mind. "There is," Maimonides reiterates many times in the *Guide*, "in truth, no relation in any respect between Him and any of His creatures." Therefore,

> the terms "knowledge," "power," "will," and "life," as applied to Him, may He be exalted, and to all those possessing knowledge, power, will and life, are purely equivocal, so that their meaning when they are predicated of Him is in no way like their meaning in other applications. (*Guide* I.56; Maimonides 1963: I.131)

We can certainly say things like "God is merciful," "God is gracious," and "God is just." We can conceive of God as subject to jealousy, hate, anger, joy, and other such emotional states. But what we are really doing when we make such predications is projecting onto God characteristics that are properly and meaningfully used only with respect to human beings, just because they are derived from our observation of human behavior.

Knowledge of God

There is, in fact, not much about God that we can know for certain, especially if knowledge is a matter of true, justified beliefs and verifiable assertions. Both the limitations of our finite minds when confronting an infinite being and God's nature as an absolutely simple unity – which rules out any distinction between substance and properties in God – preclude the possibility of making essential attributions to, and subject-predicate statements about, God. The best that we can do, really, is recognize that when we say "God exists" or "God is just" or "God is all-knowing" we are making not a positive claim but a negative one: "God is not non-existent," "God is not unjust," and "God is not ignorant."

> It is impossible that He should have affirmative attributes. For He has no "That" outside of His "What", and hence an attribute cannot be indicative of one of the two ... He cannot have accidents so that an attribute cannot be indicative of them. Accordingly, He cannot have an affirmative attribute in any respect. As for the negative attributes, they are those

that must be used in order to conduct the mind toward that which must be believed with regard to Him. (*Guide* I.58; Maimonides 1963: I.135.)

There cannot be any absence or imperfection in God. Insofar as inexistence, injustice, and ignorance are "privations," a lack of positive things – existence, justice, knowledge – what the permissible negative attributions do is, at most, "signify the negation of the privation of the attribute in question." But we need also to bear in mind that even these negative predications involve a kind of category mistake. When we say that God does not lack intelligence, the kind of intelligence that this proposition seems to imply God possesses cannot be in any way comparable to human intelligence.

In the first section of the first book (*Sefer ha-Madda*, Book of Knowledge) of the *Mishneh Torah*, the *Hilkhot Yesodei ha-Torah* (Laws of the Foundations of the Torah), Maimonides notes that it is a commandment "to love and fear this glorious and awesome God." This love arises when one contemplates the world and appreciates it as the product of God's creative activity.

> What is the path to love and fear of Him? When a person contemplates His wondrous and great deeds and creations and sees His infinite wisdom that surpasses all comparison, he will immediate love, praise, and glorify Him. (*Hilkhot Yesodei Ha-Torah* II.2)

The love of God is thus closely associated with knowledge. And the object of knowledge is, in a sense, God. However, the knowledge of God that leads to the love of God is not a direct and intimate apprehension of the nature of God, or God's "essence as it is in itself." Maimonides emphasizes to his reader that there is no question here of conceiving "the true nature of the Creator as He [truly] is" (II.8). Still, we can come to a knowledge of God's "actions" and, through them, have at least a relational and projective conception of God's character. By "God's actions," Maimonides means God's visible creation and especially God's governance of it as this is manifest in what we would now call the laws of nature and the natural phenomena they cover.

> When a person meditates on these matters and recognizes all the creations, the angels, the spheres, man, and the like, and sees the wisdom of the Holy One, blessed be He, in all these creations, he will add to his love

for God. His soul will thirst and his flesh will long with love for God, blessed be He. (*Hikhot Yesodei Ha-Torah*, IV.12)

What such a person achieves at this level is basically a command of the natural sciences, especially astronomy and physics. It is a knowledge of the workings of the cosmos, including the constitution and motions of the celestial spheres and the heavenly bodies they carry in their orbits, and the sublunar world of hylomorphic substances that these spheres govern. This is what Maimonides provisionally calls *Ma'aseh Bereshit*, the Story of Creation, as opposed to *Ma'aseh Merkaveh*, the Story of [Ezekiel's] Chariot, or the divine science.[3] (The latter, he says, "should never be expounded upon, even to a single individual, unless he is wise and capable of understanding" [*Hikhot Yesodei Ha-Torah*, IV.11]). Through careful observation of the structures and dynamics of things, from the arrangement of the stars to the organization of living bodies and study of their law-like behavior, one is led to think about God as the intelligent agent behind nature and on that basis draw certain conclusions about him. Scientific knowledge generates an appreciation and admiration of the Creator insofar as nature cannot but be taken to express that Creator's character – what we project to be his wisdom, power, purposes, and will.

However, such empirically based knowledge of God – the kind that generates the love of God with which Maimonides is concerned in these texts – remains superficial and indirect: a figurative or imaginative conception of God derived exclusively from contemplation of the world around us and the grander scheme of things but that does not capture what God is in himself. Nature and its law-like regularities, as constitutive of God's "actions," are taken to be a manifestation of, and thus a kind of evidence for, wisdom, providence, justice, and equity. While God's essence is necessarily out of reach and we cannot know anything directly (noninferentially) and in positive terms about it, we can arrive at what are essentially fictional but functional beliefs about God based on His "ways" as these are evident in the phenomena of

---

[3] It is important to note that *Ma'aseh Bereshit* is not to be taken as an account of God's activity in creating – it does not explain the ultimate origin of things from God – but only of the nature of things once God has created them. The "creation" in question is not an activity but the effect of the activity.

creation. In this way, certain qualified attributions of Him are warranted.

Likewise, in the *Guide*, as in the halakhic writings, Maimonides notes that it is at least possible for human beings to acquire a knowledge of God's ways or actions insofar as His governance of the world is discernible in the order of nature. Indeed, it is only this level of knowledge of God of which most (but not all) people are capable.[4] In the *Guide*, he does add some detail as to the way in which one is supposed to arrive at an inferential, relational conception of the divine.

> The apprehension of these [God's] actions is an apprehension of His attributes, with respect to which He is known ... Whenever one of His actions is apprehended, the attribute from which this action proceeds is predicated of Him, may He be exalted, and the name deriving from that action is applied to Him ... It is not that He possesses moral qualities, but that He performs actions resembling the actions that in us proceed from moral qualities.

Human beings typically perform actions of type φ from some state of character or motive α. Behind a charitable act there is presumed a generous or charitable motivation. Whenever God is regarded as the agent of an action that has φ-like qualities – evident either in the course of nature or in Torah – a character-state or motive similar to α is projected onto him. For example, when God is said to be "merciful," just as parents are merciful to their children,

> [i]t is not that He, may He be exalted, is affected and has compassion, but rather an action proceeds from Him that is similar to that which proceeds from a father in respect to his child and that [in the father] is attached to compassion, pity and an absolute passion. (*Guide* I.54; Maimonides 1963: I.124–5, translation modified for clarity)

What all this means is that, once again, any attribution to God, in the Bible or elsewhere, of qualities such as mercy and justice, any depiction of God as having thoughts, a will, and preferences, must be taken metaphorically, *as if* God were like us but only greater.

---

[4] The intellectually perfected person can attain a higher knowledge of God, leading to a different kind of love of God; I discuss this in Chapter 4.

> With reference to these actions [causing great calamities like floods and earthquakes], He is called *jealous and avenging and keeping anger and wrathful*, meaning that actions similar to those that proceed from us from a certain aptitude of the soul – namely, jealousy, holding fast to vengeance, hatred or anger – proceed from Him, may He be exalted, because of the deserts of those who are punished, and not because of any passion whatever. (*Guide* I.54; Maimonides 1963: I.126)

Even when we read of God issuing the *mitzvot*, handing down to Moses the commandments that are the prescriptions and prohibitions of the Torah, "the words are used accordingly by way of likening His actions to ours" (*Guide* I.65; Maimonides 1963: I.159. See also *Mishneh Torah, Hilkhot Yesodei HaTorah*, I.11).

Maimonides' attack on anthropomorphism and his insistence that God is not only not at all like us but absolutely ineffable – that what God is and how God acts is beyond anything we can meaningfully say or think – must be attractive to people of faith who, while they believe in God, are turned off by superstitious, human-like conceptions of God. Maimonides' God has no body and no mind (such as we introspectively understand what a mind is), no thoughts, feelings, or emotions. Maimonides' God is without gender, race, or anything that might make him even remotely personable and familiar. At the same time, one might doubt whether this is even a God to whom one would pray or from whom one would seek aid or comfort.

Perhaps this is just Maimonides' point.

How to Read the Bible

So, not everything that the Bible says about God should be taken at face value. And yet, the prophetic writings are, in Maimonides' view, meant to tell us *something* about God, and about many other things. The challenge when reading the Bible, then, is to know when precisely to stick with the literal reading of a term or sentence and when to adopt a figurative reading. For Maimonides, it is not only when a literal reading is awkward or hard to understand; this would be to trivialize the whole enterprise and render it rather relativistic, even subjective. What is awkward, weird, or difficult to understand for one person may not be so for another. Maimonides recognizes this, and so provides what he takes to be a clear and unambiguous method for dealing with equivocal terms in the Bible. Indeed, what is going on in those opening chapters of the *Guide* devoted to particular words is that he is laying the groundwork for his fundamental principle of biblical hermeneutics.

Maimonides summarizes the principle of his approach – and there *is* a principle – in the course of his discussion of how exactly to read the creation story of Genesis (*Bereshit*, Hebrew for "In the beginning"). He argues that there is not sufficient justification for reading the narrative of God's six-day generation of the cosmos in other than a literal way. As tempting and "easy" as a figurative reading would be, one that would be consistent with the Aristotelian view that the universe is eternal and uncreated, he notes that

> there are two causes responsible for our not doing this or believing it. One of them is ... that the deity is not a body has been demonstrated; from this it follows necessarily that everything that in its external meaning disagrees with this demonstration must be interpreted figuratively, for it is known that such texts are of necessity fit for figurative interpretation. However, the eternity of the world has not been demonstrated.

In this case, where a literal reading of the text is not falsified by a philosophical demonstration, it ought not to be rejected and the text figuratively interpreted.

The second reason why the creation story should be read in the default literal mode is that accepting that the universe was created is, unlike those corporeal descriptions of God, not contrary to faith and proper worship.

> Our belief that the deity is not a body destroys for us none of the foundations of the Law and does not give the lie to the claims of any prophet ... On the other hand, the belief in the eternity of the world the way Aristotle sees it – that is, the belief according to which the world exists in virtue of necessity, that no nature changes at all, and that the customary course of events cannot be modified with respect to anything – destroys the Law in its principle, necessarily gives the lie to every miracle, and reduces to inanity all the hopes and threats that the Law holds out. (*Guide* I.25; Maimonides 1963: II.328)[5]

---

[5] And yet, Maimonides also insists, later in the *Guide*, that "not everything mentioned in the Torah concerning the Account of the Beginning is to be taken in its external [literal] sense as the

Maimonides' guiding principle for the reading of the Bible thus comprises two rules:

1. The default mode of reading any passage in the Bible is the literal reading.
2. One is justified in departing from the default literal reading only when that reading is either (a) inconsistent with a demonstrated philosophical or theological truth, or (b) detrimental to faith and worship.

The demand for a figurative or metaphorical reading is not meant to apply only to such things as parables, allegories or fables, which are the obvious candidates for a nonliteral approach, but also to even the most simple predicative sentences, especially those involving God. The reason why the Bible's talk of God's "head," "hands," "face," and other bodily elements should not be read literally is because, as we know from purely logical reasoning, God cannot possibly have a body. The tenet "God is one" is the most important principle in all of Judaism. It is an essential part of the central Jewish prayer, the *Shema*: "Hear, O Israel, the Lord our God, the Lord is One." And, as we have seen, it can be rationally demonstrated that a being that is essentially one cannot be corporeal. Because corporeal or material beings can always be divided into parts, they are not simple and true unities. Moreover, according to the Aristotelian metaphysics that Maimonides favors, any *corporeal* substance is constituted out of matter and form. A statue, to take a very basic example, comprises both its marble matter and the shape imposed on it by the sculptor. A corporeal substance is thus composite, not simple. "There is no profession of unity unless the doctrine of God's corporeality is denied. For a body cannot be one, but is composed of matter and form, which by definition are two; it is also divisible, subject to partition" (*Guide* I.35; Maimonides 1963: I.81). Thus, a (literal) reading of a Scriptural passage that involves attributing a corporeal

---

vulgar imagine ... For the external sense of these texts leads either to a grave corruption of the imagination and to giving vent to evil opinions with regard to the deity, or to an absolute denial of the action of the deity and to disbelief in the foundations of the Law" (II.29; Maimonides 1963: 346–7). Should the creation story, or at least parts of it, then, be read figuratively and regarded as a parable? Only if, as this passage shows, doing so is justified by Maimonides' rule of interpretation.

nature to God runs up against a rigorously demonstrated truth about God and, for that reason, ought to be rejected. The Bible must be read in a way that accommodates the incorporeality doctrine. Any mention of God's "eye" is to be taken as referring to his watchfulness, his providence or his intellectual apprehension; while talk of God's "heart" is to be understood as referring to his thought or his opinion.

More generally, whenever a literal reading of a word or passage in the Bible would carry a meaning that is inconsistent with an absolutely certain philosophical, theological, or other "speculative" truth, the word or passage must be read figuratively or metaphorically. On the other hand, when a literal reading, no matter how implausible or counterintuitive it may seem, does not contradict any demonstrated truth, it should be preserved.

Maimonides intends this criterion to be taken in the strictest manner. He distinguishes between what is demonstrated and what is supported only by "strong arguments" (*Guide* I.4; Maimonides 1963: I.28). A true demonstration begins with absolutely certain premises or first principles, and then proceeds through deduction to its conclusion. The argument must be not only valid – with the conclusion following necessarily from the premises, even if those premises are false – but sound, whereby the premises are true and thus guarantee the truth of any conclusion validly derived from them. "The rejection of the doctrine of the corporeality of God," he notes, "is a matter of demonstration and is necessary for belief" (*Guide* I.28; Maimonides 1963: I.60). By contrast, while there may be good reasons, and maybe even "strong arguments," to believe that the cosmos is eternal – or so some Aristotelians thought – such a claim (as Maimonides insists several times throughout the *Guide*) has not been, and cannot be, rigorously demonstrated. Then again, Maimonides concedes, neither can it be demonstrated that the cosmos was created. No philosophical proof can definitively establish the one account or the other. He does, in fact, regard creation as the far more *probable* opinion, one that, given the empirical evidence – especially the uneven distribution of stars across the heavens, which points in favor of their being placed by an intelligent agent rather than by brute necessity – should be accepted as "correct." Be that as it may, in the absence of any clear and distinct demonstration against creation, a figurative reading of the creation chapters of Genesis is not warranted.

In short, no matter how odd or otherwise problematic a passage may seem, if a literal reading is not logically incompatible with a demonstrated truth – and, moreover, does not undermine faith – that must be its proper meaning. Now it may be difficult to understand how an eternal God, who stands outside all temporal categories, can create something in time. But the mere challenge of making theological or metaphysical sense of this is insufficient to justify reading these parts of Genesis in anything but a literal way. Moreover, the literal reading of the creation story is religiously safe, and cannot be disqualified by any ill effect it might have on faith. "Know that with a belief in the creation of the world in time, all the miracles become possible and the Law becomes possible, and all questions that may be asked on this subject vanish" (*Guide* II.25; Maimonides 1963: II.329).

Biblical Rationalism

Maimonides' arch-rationalist approach to the interpretation of the Bible – where reason is the touchstone of meaning – is not without precedent in Jewish thought. Scriptural rationalism is found in a particularly clear form in some early Jewish texts in the Karaite tradition. Thus, Jacob al-Kirkisani (fl. ca. 930–40, in Mesopotamia), in his *Book of Lights*, insists that

> Scripture as a whole is to be interpreted literally, except where literal interpretation may involve something objectionable or imply a contradiction ... Thus we are compelled to say that the verse, "And they saw the God of Israel ... "(Exodus 24:10), must not be understood literally, and does not signify seeing with one's eyes, since it is contrary to reason to assume that the Creator may be perceived by man's senses.[6]

It is evident that the criterion for what is an "objectionable" reading of the text is, for al-Kirkisani, a matter of what is reasonable. Similarly, Japheth ben Ali ha-Levi (fl. second half of tenth century) writes that "we are not justified in setting aside the literal meaning of the word of God

---

[6] See Nemoy 1932: 60.

or of His prophets except where that literal meaning is hindered or precluded as being contradicted by reason or by a clear idea."[7]

This hermeneutic method, with philosophy (broadly understood) setting the parameters for interpretation, finds perhaps its earliest systematic expression not in a Karaite work, however, but in a highly authoritative source: *The Book of Beliefs and Opinions*, by Saadya ben Joseph (882–942), the *gaon* or head of the rabbinical academy in Sura, Babylonia. Saadya first broaches the topic when he asks how one is to know whether a person is a true prophet and that what he proclaims is indeed divine prophecy. In the first place, he answers, prophetic messages are accompanied by "certain signs and wondrous miracles." Just as important, however, is the fact that *what* is communicated by the prophetic message is rational, acceptable to and confirmed by reason.

> The basis of our belief in the mission of Moses is not solely the miracles and marvels that he performed. The reason for our believing in him, and in every other prophet, is rather the fact that he first called upon us to do what is proper. Then, when we had heard his appeal and we saw that it was proper, we demanded from him miracles in support of it and, when he performed them, we believed in him. If, however, we had felt that the appeal that he made at the beginning was not proper, we would not have demanded any miracles from him, because miracles are of no account in supporting the unacceptable.[8]

The measure for what is "proper" and "acceptable" is what is rational. Reason has absolute authority here and cannot be overruled even by the performance of a miracle.

> The same procedure is to be followed in the case of every claimant of prophecy. If he says to us, "My Lord commands you to fast today", we ask him for a sign in support of his mission, and when he shows it to us, we accept it and fast. If, however, he were to say to us, "My Lord commands you to commit adultery and steal", or "He informs you that He is about to bring a flood of water upon the world", or "He makes it known to you that He created heaven and earth thoughtlessly while He was asleep", we would not ask him for any sign, since what he called upon us to do is not sanctioned by either reason or tradition.[9]

---

[7] See Sirat 1985: 47.   [8] Saadya 1948: 163.   [9] Saadya 1948: 164.

While Saadya's mention of "tradition" in this passage might seem to offer a second, nonrational criterion, it is clear from his discussion of Scripture that that tradition is itself informed by proper reason.

Saadya insists that every statement that is found in the Bible is to be read in its literal sense unless one of four conditions obtain. First, a literal reading might contradict what is clearly known from sense experience. Thus, Eve could not literally have been "the mother of all living beings," since it is obvious that oxen and lions are not the offspring of a woman.

Second, sometimes a literal reading is "rendered impossible" by another, non-negotiable text elsewhere in Scripture that is explicitly inconsistent with it; reconciling these two texts will thus require a figurative reading of at least one of them. In Deuteronomy 6:16, God says, "You must not challenge the Lord your God, as you challenged him at Massah," but in Malachi 3:10 God says, "Put me to the proof . . . and see if I do not open windows in the sky and pour a blessing on you." Saadya suggests that the two statements can be made to agree by reading the first one as referring only to challenges that question God's power to do a certain thing, not those that are really just requests to perform a miracle.

Third – and here Saadya may be referring to something like Maimonides' condition of consistency with the faith – if rabbinic tradition has attached a certain figurative interpretation to the text in question, then it should be interpreted according to that tradition and not literally. Although Scripture says "Forty stripes he may give him" (Deuteronomy 25:3), the rabbis have laid it down that only thirty-nine stripes are to be administered, and thus the biblical text represents just a rough way of saying that there should be thirty-nine stripes.

Finally, and most important for our purposes, Saadya insists that a figurative reading of Scripture is justified, even required, if a literal reading is contrary to something that is known for certain by reason. He notes, for example, that a literal reading of the statement "For the Lord thy God is a devouring fire, a jealous God" (Deuteronomy 4:24) is ruled out on rational grounds. "Fire is something created and defective, for it is subject to extinction. Hence it is logically inadmissable that God resemble it. We must, therefore, impute to this statement the meaning that God's punishment is like a consuming fire."[10]

---

[10] Saadya 1948: 266.

Prophecy

Behind Maimonides' commitment to a rationalist principle of interpretation is his understanding of who the prophetic authors of the Bible were and what gifts they possessed. He regards prophecy, no less than philosophy, as essentially the communication of theological, metaphysical, natural, and moral truths. The prophet has a special skill, however, one that distinguishes him from the run-of-the-mill philosopher: he is able to translate those abstract truths into concrete terms and communicate them in imaginative and edifying narrative form.

The prophet has a lot in common with the philosopher – he is, in fact, very much a philosopher, a person given to informed speculation on the natures of things. What this means, on Maimonides' account, is that the content of what an authentic prophet proclaims comes to him as an "intellectual overflow" or emanation of knowledge from the higher, "separate" intellects of the cosmos and, ultimately, from God. What he grasps and then communicates, therefore, cannot fail to be true.

> Know that the true reality and quiddity of prophecy consists in its being an overflow overflowing from God ... through the intermediation of the Active Intellect [the "separate" or angelic intellect that governs the sublunary realm], toward the rational faculty in the first place and thereafter toward the imaginative faculty. ... [Prophecy] is not something that may be attained solely through perfection in the speculative sciences and through improvement of moral habits, even if all of them have become as fine and good as can be. There still is needed in addition the highest possible degree of perfection of the imaginative faculty. (*Guide* II.36; Maimonides 1963: II.369)

This overflow of knowledge from God is the epistemic complement to the overflow of being from God that, ontologically, accounts for creation. "The world derives from the overflow of God and He has caused to overflow to it everything in it that is produced in time. In the same way it is said that He caused His knowledge to overflow to the prophets" (*Guide* II.12; Maimonides 1963: II.279).

The prophet is, thus, not only of superb moral character, well above other people in his manner of living, but like the philosopher he has achieved perfection in his intellectual or rational faculties. He is prepared to receive and understand the content of that divine cognitive overflow. For this reason, there is a sense in which prophetic utterances and writings are of the same fundamentally rational nature and have the same epistemological stature as straightforward philosophical statements. The only significant difference between the philosopher and the prophet is that perfection in the imaginative faculty that the prophet also enjoys. This is what allows him to have compelling dreams and visions, including about the future, and the capacity to weave the intellectual material into engaging narratives that make speculative truths accessible to the multitude and inspire them. What the prophet communicates, then, is, in its substance, true and rational knowledge. This means that reason will therefore be the key to interpreting prophetic writings. We must read the Bible as a source of truths, for that is what the prophetic authors are seeking to convey, even if they sometimes wrap those truths in vibrant, metaphorical language that will appeal to our embodied natures. Therefore, if a particular reading of a prophetic text cannot possibly be accepted as true – philosophically or rationally true – then that cannot be a correct reading.

Spinoza's Critique of Maimonides' Bible Hermeneutics

Maimonides' approach to reading the Bible was not uncontroversial, even within Judaism. Some rabbis favoring biblical literalism and at least allowing for, if not actually encouraging, an anthropomorphic, even corporeal, conception of God attacked the *Guide*. Maimonides' spare, "philosophical" conception of a distant, unknowable God, they feared, would alienate the unphilosophical multitude in search of a more personal deity. Maimonides' son Avraham responded to these critics on his father's behalf and accused them of encouraging gross idolatry.[11]

The historically most significant critic of Maimonides' Bible hermeneutics, however, was the seventeenth-century philosopher Bento (Baruch, Benedictus) de Spinoza (1632–1677). Spinoza was born and educated in the Amsterdam Portuguese-Jewish community, but in 1656, at the age of twenty-three, he was put under *herem* (banned or ostracized) by its leaders for his "horrifying heresies" and "atrocious deeds."

---

[11] Avraham ben Rambam 1953: 52–55.

He stands in a fascinatingly complex relationship to the Jewish rationalist tradition that precedes him. On the one hand, he was that tradition's most systematic critic, especially on matters of theology. On the other hand, there can be no question that, despite the many other influences on Spinoza's thought – including the ancient Stoics and fellow early modern philosophers such as René Descartes and Thomas Hobbes – his moral philosophy stands at the apex of the rationalist trend best represented in Jewish philosophy by Maimonides.[12]

In the inventory of Spinoza's possessions made by a Dutch notary after the philosopher's death in 1677, there was a substantial library of 160 items. Among the works of ancient philosophy (including Aristotle's *Opera* and Epictetus's *Encheiridion*), Hebrew and Latin Bibles, ancient Greek and Latin poetry and drama (including Homer's *Iliad*, poems by Ovid, tragedies by Seneca, and comedies by Plautus), a Passover *haggadah*, and works of contemporary philosophy (including no fewer than seven volumes of Descartes, a copy of Hobbes's *De cive*, and some treatises by the scientist Robert Boyle), there are in fact very few works of Jewish *philosophy* (as opposed to Torah commentaries and other rabbinic writings). Spinoza did own a Spanish translation of Leone Ebreo's *Dialoghi d'Amore* (Dialogues on Love), but – much to our surprise – no copy of anything by Levi ben Gershom (Gersonides), an important fourteenth-century rabbi and philosopher who was something of an unorthodox Maimonidean, despite the fact that Spinoza was clearly familiar with that philosopher's works.

Equally surprising is the fact that in the inventory there is one, and only one, book by Maimonides. It is not a volume of the *Mishneh Torah* or of the *Commentary on the Mishnah*. Rather, as we would hope and expect, it is the *Guide of the Perplexed*. And unlike his copy of Leone's *Dialoghi*, what Spinoza owned was not a Spanish translation of the *Guide* – Spanish was the language of high literature among the Portuguese Jews of Amsterdam – but rather Samuel Ibn Tibbon's original Hebrew text, a translation from the Arabic authorized by Maimonides himself. Spinoza had the 1515 edition published in Venice by the Bragadin firm. (This

---

[12] On Spinoza's relationship to medieval Jewish philosophy, see the essays in Nadler 2014.

family was a prominent publisher of Hebrew texts, and in 1550 one of the sons, Alvise, would also bring out an edition of Maimonides' *Mishneh Torah*.)

There can be no doubt that Spinoza had his copy of the *Guide* beside him as he worked on his *Theological-Political Treatise*, which he published in 1670. Spinoza wrote this bold and "scandalous" work – one overwrought critic called it "a book forged in hell by the devil himself" – because he was greatly troubled by the increasing power of ecclesiastics in civic affairs. He regarded especially the political influence of conservative Reformed theologians and preachers in Holland's governance as a serious threat to the liberal, secular, and tolerant ideals of the Dutch Republic and the "freedom to philosophize." Because these religious leaders wielded the Bible and their authority as the true interpreters of God's word to compel submission to their orders, Spinoza thought that the best way to undermine their social and political influence was to cut the Bible down to size.

In the *Treatise*, Spinoza rejects the idea that the Bible was literally authored by God. Spinoza's God (*Deus*) is Nature (*Natura*), and thus cannot write or dictate anything. The Bible as we have it is, rather, the work of human beings writing over generations in very particular historical and political circumstances. Thus, Spinoza concludes, Scripture, like any work of human literature, must be interpreted on its own terms and not by reference to any absolute standards outside the text and its authors' personal histories. In particular, the type of exegesis proposed by Maimonides is, for Spinoza, illegitimate insofar as it goes beyond Scripture itself – to an external canon of philosophy, rationality, or truth – in order to interpret Scripture. "To know whether Moses believed that God is a fire, we must in no way infer our answer from the fact that this sentence [taken literally] agrees with reason or is contrary to it. Instead, we must rely only on other statements Moses himself made."[13] In other words, there is an important distinction between the *meaning* of Scripture – what the book says, that is, what the author intends to convey – which is what one is after when interpreting any literary text, and what is philosophically or historically *true*.

---

[13] *Theological-Political Treatise*, VII; Spinoza 2016: 174.

We are concerned only with the meaning of the utterances, not with their truth. Indeed, we must take great care, so long as we are looking for the meaning of Scripture, not to be predisposed by our own reasoning, insofar as it is founded on the principles of natural knowledge (not to mention our own prejudices). In order not to confuse the true meaning with the truth of things, we must seek that meaning solely from linguistic usage, or from reasoning which recognizes no other foundation than Scripture.[14]

Much of what Scripture relates is *not*, in fact, true, no more so than what is related by any other work of human literature. When we read a novel – say, *Emma*, by Jane Austen – we do not decide on the interpretation of a passage in this work of fiction by appealing to what may or may not be objectively (scientifically, philosophically, psychologically) true in the world outside the novel and its author's life and projects. Rather, we rely on other things that have been happening in the story – for example, we interpret Emma's behavior in this or that instance by what we already know of her character. We may also bring in things we know about Austen herself, what she thought of the milieu in which she lived, her social circle, and so on; as part of the "history" of the text, these are all relevant factors in our hermeneutical endeavor. For Spinoza, if what Scripture states does, in some cases, happen to be true, it is not, despite what Maimonides says, *necessarily* the case that what it states is true.

Spinoza, who was a close reader of Maimonides' *Guide*, agreed with part of Maimonides' account of prophecy: the ancient prophets were individuals of outstanding ethical character and comportment and powerful imaginations. But, he insists, they were not philosophers or especially learned; many of them were rustic individuals who were hardly educated at all. Thus, there is no guarantee that what they have to say on any topic other than moral living and the love of God is the truth on that matter. In one of his typically bold statements, Spinoza insists that "it is one thing to understand Scripture and the mind of the Prophets, and another to understand the mind of God, that is, the truth of the matter itself."[15] Scripture is not by its nature a source of

---

[14] *Theological-Political Treatise*, VII; Spinoza 2016: 173.
[15] *Theological-Political Treatise*, XII; Spinoza 2016: 253.

knowledge, least of all true knowledge about God, the heavens, or even human nature (although it *is* a source of knowledge about what its various writers believed on these matters). It is not, in other words, philosophy or science. "We are not at all bound to believe them concerning purely speculative matters ... we really should not seek knowledge of natural and spiritual things from them."[16]

It follows, then, that the principles of reason, the touchstone of truth, must not serve as our guide in interpreting Scripture. Or, to put it in Spinozistic terms, just as philosophy does not have to answer to theology – the discipline for discovering the word of God through the prophetic writings – and conform to its dictates, so theology does not have to answer to philosophy. The universal and "clear" moral message of Scripture – that one should love God above all, and one's neighbor as oneself – does, indeed, agree with reason in the sense that our rational faculties approve of it; we could even discover this truth for ourselves, without the Bible's help (as Spinoza shows in his philosophical masterpiece, the *Ethics*). But *that* the Bible teaches such a message is not an a priori certainty, as it is for Maimonides; it can be discovered only through the "historical" hermeneutical method applied to the biblical text.

Spinoza is certainly not a biblical literalist. He allows that sometimes we really have no alternative to adopting a figurative or metaphorical reading of a passage. But when, precisely, is a figurative reading called for if not when a literal reading conflicts with a rationally demonstrated truth? Spinoza's answer is: only when a literal reading is in clear violation of "the basic principles derived from the study of Scripture" – that is, only when a literal reading is inconsistent with a sufficient number of other evident statements in the text and stands in the way of clarifying the intentions or beliefs of the author. Thus, the question when reading biblical passages about God is not whether God, in metaphysical truth, has a body or is susceptible to passions such as anger and jealousy but whether or not a particular prophet believed these things and intended to convey that message through his writings. And we can only answer this question by examining those writings themselves, as well as the biographical, historical, political, and religious circumstances of their

---

[16] *Theological-Political Treatise*, II; Spinoza 2016: 100, 109.

composition. Thus, Moses (assuming him to be the author) proclaims in the Torah that God has no resemblance to visible things, and yet he also likens God to fire. One needs to inquire, then, as to which of these passages needs to be read metaphorically, regardless of the rationality or irrationality of the proposition or the belief that would consequently be attributed to the prophet. If linguistic usage in biblical Hebrew suggests that the word "fire" does not have any meaning besides a literal one, then the other passages that say that God has no resemblance to things in heaven or on the earth need to be read figuratively.

Spinoza says that one needs to keep in mind that the purpose of Scripture is not to communicate speculative truths but to compel obedience to God's law, that is, to the command to love God and your fellow human beings and treat them with justice, charity, and loving-kindness. The narratives of the Torah and other writings of the Hebrew Bible – the episodes they relate about God and human beings, the events of nature – are a reflection of the beliefs, values, preconceptions, and purposes of their authors and especially what they presumed would most appeal to their audience. The prophets adopted various literary devices to convey a simple moral and religious message and to inspire readers to obey it. The *truth* of the resulting propositions and stories is irrelevant to this goal, and even to the value of Scripture itself. Sometimes a well-crafted fiction can do all the necessary morally inspirational work. Indeed, this, for Spinoza, is precisely what constitutes the "divinity" and "sacredness" of Scripture. "What is called sacred and divine is what is destined for the practice of piety and religion. It will be sacred only so long as men use it in a religious manner . . . Scripture is sacred and its statements divine just as long as it moves men to devotion toward God."[17]

Spinoza concludes that "Maimonides' method is utterly useless." By making philosophy the touchstone of interpretation, Maimonides supposes that

> we are permitted to explain and twist the words of Scripture according to our preconceived opinions, to deny their literal meaning (even when that meaning is most clearly perceived or most explicit), and to change it into any other meaning we like.

---

[17] *Theological-Political Treatise*, XII; Spinoza 2016: 250–1.

In an even stronger vein, Spinoza insists that the Maimonidean approach is positively detrimental to the Bible's effectiveness in motivating obedience to God's law. If Maimonides is right, then most ordinary people cannot have any access to much of the meaning of Scripture. "His method completely takes away all the certainty the common people can have about the meaning of Scripture from a natural reading of it." The multitude do not have the philosophical training and speculative knowledge that would allow them to evaluate whether the reading of this or that biblical passage is consistent with what is demonstrably true; they would therefore have no idea when to stick with a literal interpretation and when to opt for a figurative one. Spinoza's judgment is that "we condemn Maimonides' opinion as not only useless, but harmful and absurd."[18]

Why Read the Bible?

There are many reasons why we read the Hebrew Bible. It is, of course, a highly entertaining work of literature, great storytelling full of drama, tragic and comic. It has spectacular action, a good deal of violence, and vivid characters (including the character named "God") whose ordeals – their relationships and emotional lives; their ambitions, achievements, mistakes, and failures; their love and enmity – are both a cause of wonder and remarkably familiar.

The Bible is also, for many – and not just people of faith – a source of inspiration and enlightenment. When Abraham hears God's command to sacrifice his child Isaac; when Hagar hears from Sarah that she and her son Ishmael must go away into the wilderness; when David, lusting after Bathsheba, sends her husband Uriah to his death in battle; when Job finally complains about the injustice of his sufferings: these are all morally complex and terribly moving situations, often (but not always) imposed upon individuals by circumstances beyond their control. We may turn from philosophy to literature to see the ways in which ordinary (and extraordinary) people wrestle with ethical and spiritual challenges. This can be an edifying experience for us and an important

---

[18] *Theological-Political Treatise*, VII; Spinoza 2016: 190.

part of our moral education as we critically examine our own beliefs and seek clarity on our values.

Perhaps in this sense the Bible is, for Spinoza, a source of "truth," and we read it for whatever lessons – about human nature, about the meaning of life, etc. – may be found there. For similar insights we may read Miguel de Cervantes, Shakespeare, George Eliot, Fyodor Dostoyevski, Virginia Woolf, and a wealth of other works of world literature. By Spinoza's criteria, if these novels and plays move us to treat others with justice, charity, and loving-kindness – or at least reveal to us why people sometimes fail to do so – then they, too, are divine and sacred.

Maimonides, as we have seen, would take this one step further: the Bible most definitely *is* a source of truth just because its authors were intellectually and imaginatively gifted philosophers. In his view, if we read the Bible properly – when we understand when to take its passages literally and when to interpret them metaphorically – we are able to glean from its narratives objective, universal truths about God, the world, and human nature, as well as an understanding of the social and ethical codes by which we should live. Spinoza would agree with at least part of this. For the most part, we should read the Bible as we would read any novel – to follow the author's story and discover whatever he or she meant to say. If there is something *true* to be learned as well, something of which reason approves, it would be the clear and unadulterated moral message that can be found expressed throughout all the narratives of Scripture: Love your fellow human beings as yourself.

CHAPTER 3

Why Bad Things Happen to Good People

In the prologue to the Book of Job, we are told that the eponymous protagonist of the story is a blameless and upright man (in Hebrew, *tam ve-yashar*), that he fears God and turns away from wrongdoing. When Job's tribulations begin, he accepts them unshaken in his faith and unwilling to speak ill of God. "If we accept good from God, shall we not accept evil?" (Job 2:10). As his losses mount, however, it is, ultimately, all too much even for him. When Job is finally overcome by his suffering, when he has been robbed of everything that was dear to him, when all seems lost, he raises his voice to complain to God about the way he, a righteous individual, has been treated. While Job recognizes God's wisdom and power, he nonetheless questions God's justice. God, he insists, "rains blows on me without cause ... He destroys blameless and wicked alike" (Job 9:17–22).

The story of Job offers the first real presentation in Jewish literature of what has come to be known as "the problem of evil." To generate this philosophical problem, a number of conceptual and empirical ingredients are required. First, of course, there must be a God, and that God is both the creator of the world we inhabit and a providential agent who watches over things. If there is no God, there is no problem of evil, at least in the traditional sense. Why would we expect impersonal nature to be anything but thoroughly indifferent to our fate and well-being?

Second, there must be evil, or at least the appearance of evil, in God's creation. Regardless of what kind of evil we want to focus on – the seventeenth-century philosopher Gottfried Wilhelm Leibniz distinguished between physical, metaphysical, and moral evils – there must nonetheless be some order of imperfection in the world, especially relative to human beings. Sometimes the imperfection will be the sins committed by moral agents – we lie, cheat, steal, and murder. In other cases, it will consist in the suffering of the virtuous and innocent and the flourishing of the wicked. Congenital disabilities, natural disasters, and tragically untimely deaths are all undeniable features of the world. In and of itself, this is troubling and a source of pathos, but it is still not philosophically problematic. It becomes problematic – and generates the set of questions that constitute the problem of evil – only when taken in conjunction with a number of claims about God, claims that also prevent any kind of simplistic solution to those questions.

First, God is omnipotent; that is, God can do whatever God wants to do, and God's will is, at least absolutely speaking, of infinite scope. This prevents one from saying that God knows and cares about the evils in His creation but cannot do anything about them. Second, God is omniscient; God knows everything, including the alleged defects in his work. This forecloses resolving the problem by saying that God could (and would) do something about the evils in his creation if only He knew about them; and since he obviously has not done anything about them, he must not know about them. Third, God is benevolent and just; God wills only what is good and watches over his creation with righteousness. This bars a resolution of the conundrum by arguing that God knows about the evils and is capable of preventing them, but simply does not care to do so. How, then, can we reconcile the existence of pain, imperfection, sin, and undeserved suffering in the world with the fact that the world was created by a just, wise, good, omniscient, omnipotent, and free God?

Leibniz coined a word to refer to the philosophical attempt to answer this question. A "theodicy" – from the ancient Greek words *theos* (God) and *diké* (justice) – takes seriously the tension between these various metaphysical, moral, and theological claims and seeks to provide a justification of God's ways. Job's friends engage in theodicy when they come to him to offer rationalizations for why he has been visited with such disaster. Assuming that there must be a sufficient and satisfying explanation for Job's situation, they argue that it is either because of his or his relations' iniquities or because God has, in his infinite wisdom, some other reason that transcends our cognitive powers. Eliphaz the Temanite suggests that if Job is suffering, it must be because he has sinned somewhere along the way. God is just, he claims – with a recognizable, even conventional kind of justice according to which virtue is rewarded and vice in punished – and a just God does not inflict undeserved punishment. Eliphaz later broadens this idea and insists that the metaphysical distance between the human being and God implies that the human being is essentially corrupt and therefore deserving of whatever evils God brings his way.

> What is frail man that he should be innocent, or any child of woman that he should be justified? If God puts no trust in his holy ones, and the heavens are not innocent in his sight, how much less so is man, who is loathsome and rotten? (Job 15:14–16)

Another one of Job's friends, foreshadowing a type of theodicy that will become quite prominent in Jewish philosophical thinking about evil, believes that our judgments about God's justice should not be limited to what we see in some narrow slice of this life, where it often happens that the righteous suffer and the wicked prosper. If Job is truly innocent, Bildad the Shuhite suggests, then he should consider that he will be rewarded in the long term – not just in this life, which for the righteous is long and eventually prosperous, but especially in what will come to him after his death:

> It is the wicked whose light is extinguished, from whose fire no flame will rekindle; the light fades in his tent, and his lamp dies down and fails him ... He roots beneath dry up, and above, his branches wither. His memory vanishes from the face of the earth, and he leaves no name in the world. He is driven from light into darkness and banished from the land of the living. He leaves no issue or offspring among his people, no survivor in his earthly home. (Job 18:5–20)

The ultimate fate of the wicked, despite their temporary flourishing, is oblivion; they are, in the end, "cut off." The implication is that the righteous person, on the other hand, while he may suffer for a time in this life, should enjoy the knowledge that the fruits and rewards of his virtue will be great in the end, and will persist long after he is gone from this world. As Zophar the Naamathite insists, "the triumph of the wicked is short-lived, the glee of the godless lasts but a moment. Though he stands high as heaven, and his head touches the clouds, he will be swept away utterly, like his own dung" (Job 20:5–7).

3 Why Bad Things Happen to Good People

From the perspective of theodicy, the Book of Job ends on an ambiguous and, ultimately, unsatisfying note. The speech by Elihu, after the other friends are done, seems at first to represent a supreme defense of God's justice – a justice that, like Eliphaz's justice, is couched in simple, comprehensible, even human terms. "Far be it from God to do evil or the Almighty to play false! For he pays a man according to his work and sees that he gets what his conduct deserves. The truth is, God does no wrong, the Almighty does not pervert justice" (Job 34:10–12). And yet, Elihu ends by appealing to God's metaphysical and epistemological transcendence, and (by implication) the inscrutability of his ways: "God is so great that we cannot know him" (36:26). One must have faith that God is just, but with a justice that is beyond our notion of justice and comprehension and such that he cannot be called to account. God's own, final speech in the narrative seems to confirm Elihu's sentiments. After pointing out the majesty and wonder of creation and the ultimate mystery and incomprehensibility of the world, God puts an end to the discussion: "Can you deny that I am just or put me in the wrong that you may be right?" (40:8). God is just, but with a justice that cannot be explained in terms drawn from human justice.[1]

Despite this final anti-rationalism about divine justice, the Book of Job was the spur for a long rationalist tradition in Jewish thought on the problem of evil, including Maimonides.[2] These thinkers, just because of their rationalism, faced a particular challenge when addressing the problem of evil. On one hand, they were committed to the idea that the problem did have an answer, that the humble skepticism or appeal to faith that closes the Book of Job is not the last word on the matter. An explanation can indeed be given for the suffering of the virtuous and the prospering of the vicious. There are accessible reasons why bad things happen to good people and good things to bad people. It is something we can understand. On the other hand, not even the most convinced rationalist of the medieval period was willing to say that God's reasons are completely transparent to human understanding, that we can know

---
[1] There is a large number of studies of the Book of Job as theodicy; for a recent philosophical account, see Leaman 1995.
[2] For a discussion of some aspects of the commentary tradition on Job in Jewish philosophy, see Eisen 2004; and Goodman's essay in Saadia 1988: 28–92.

the deepest secrets of divine wisdom and find therein the theodicean answer we seek. (It would take a Spinoza to make such an audacious claim, in part by dismissing the whole problem of theodicy as based on a false and superstitious conception of God.)

Another factor is the rationalist's need to avoid the anthropomorphization of God. Maimonides, as we have seen, countered attempts to portray God as a personal agent. He was thus forced to explain divine providence without resorting to a human-like God who regards each individual situation in its particularity and actively engages in the distribution of reward and punishment in a deliberate way – fending off dangers from the righteous and hurling thunderbolts upon the vicious.

All of this is well captured by Maimonides' approach to the problem. Without personalizing God or allowing that God's wisdom is sufficiently accessible to finite minds so that the resolution of the problem can be found therein, he does insist that we can understand why bad things happen to good people, and why the distribution of goods and evils, in this world and in the world to come, as unjust as it may appear, is as it is.

Evil

In the *Guide*, Maimonides first considers the nature of evil itself. Like many other medieval thinkers, he rejects Manicheanism – the view that good and evil are equally positive realities and that the world results from the struggle between them – and argues that evil is not some actual being.[3] Evil is nothing real. Whatever is real and caused by God is good. "All evils are privations," he insists, and are constituted by the lack or absence of some goodness or perfection. At one point, in fact, Maimonides seems close to dismissing evil altogether as an illusion due to our anthropocentric way of looking at the world (*Guide* III.12; Maimonides 1963: II.442–3). We think things are bad in themselves, a blight upon God's creation, just because they are bad *for us*. Still, he recognizes that no ontological or epistemological sleight of hand will really make evil as a phenomenon disappear and obviate the need for a theodicy.

---

[3] For a general discussion of Maimonides on the problem of evil, see Leaman 1995, chapter 4.

With respect to human beings, all evils/privations are grounded in our matter. The bodily aspect of our existence is the source not only of our basic exposure to physical harms but also of our base desires, wicked impulses, and ignorance. Maimonides divides human evil into three categories. First, there are the evils that happen to us in the ordinary course of nature just because, as material beings, we are subject to the elements. Bodily infirmities, injuries, even death itself are unavoidable in our corporeal human condition. Second, there are the evils that human beings inflict upon one another because of their urges and inclinations: deceit, theft, tyrannical domination, murder. Third, there are the evils that an individual brings upon himself through his own actions. "This kind is consequent upon all vices," Maimonides says, and includes intemperate eating and drinking, "excessive copulation," and the doing of bad things unto others. This species of evil brings harm not only to the body but to the soul as well, especially as its moral qualities are affected by the temperament of the body (*Guide* III.12; Maimonides 1963: II.443–5). His point here is not unlike a claim that Socrates makes while in prison awaiting execution, namely, that doing wrong harms not only the wronged person but, even more so, the wrongdoer, and in his most important part: his soul.[4] Regardless of whether evil is categorized ontologically as something real and positive or a mere negation or lack, then, there can be no denying that these three kinds of evil occur and have a deleterious effect on human existence and flourishing.

Theodicy, Take One: Consider the Whole

One solution to the problem of evil that Maimonides adopts involves what might be called the "consider the whole" approach. According to this strategy, any concerns about divine justice generated by evil in the world are due to our having adopted too narrow a view of things – for example, by looking only at certain features of the world and not others. We can therefore alleviate those concerns by broadening our perspective and considering more or different aspects of creation, even the whole of creation itself. We will then see that the world is, on the whole, good.

---

[4] See Plato, *Crito* 47d–e.

This strategy can take two forms, depending upon just how we are supposed to broaden our perspective and regard the world holistically. While one variety asks for a quantitative expansion of vision, the other requires a qualitative reorientation.

Maimonides initially takes up the theodicean challenge by responding to the complaint, "which often occurs to the imagination of the multitude," that the three species of evil are ubiquitous, that the world created by God is predominantly bad, and "there are more evils in the world than there are good things." Understood in this way, the problem of evil is a quantitative problem, and thus its solution is to be found in a proper reckoning of the number of good things versus the number of evil things. "Consider the whole," on this reading, means look at a greater sampling of the world's phenomena and you will see that, as a matter of fact, the premise of the complaint is false and the number of good things is greater than the number of evil things. Thus, with respect to at least the first two species of evil, Maimonides argues that a true accounting reveals that they do not occur as often as the multitude believe. The evils that we suffer because of our material nature

> are very few and occur only seldom. For you will find cities existing for thousands of years that have never been flooded or burned. Also, thousands of people are born in perfect health whereas the birth of an infirm human being is an anomaly, or at least... such an individual is very rare; for they do not form a hundredth or even a thousandth part of those born in good health.

Similarly, with respect to the evils that we inflict upon one another, he argues that while they may be more numerous than those of the first variety, they nonetheless "do not form the majority of occurrences upon the earth taken as a whole"; rather, they become common only in extreme circumstances, such as war and times of political upheaval (*Guide* III.12; Maimonides 1963: II.444).

While this version of the "consider the whole" strategy could, in theory, afford a reply to the charge that the world created by God is *predominantly* evil and that the bad things outnumber the good – in fact they do not, is the claim – it is ultimately an unsatisfying theodicy. First, it can lead to an unresolvable numbers game, with endless disputes about how many good things there are versus how many bad things there are, fueled by disagreements about which things are to be categorized as good and which are to be categorized as bad. Second, even if the quantitative approach does effectively respond to the charge that the world is *mostly* evil, it leaves unanswered the primary question of the problem of evil: Why is there *any* evil at all in a world created by a wise, benevolent and all-powerful God? Could not that God have created a world that is nothing but good, with no imperfections whatsoever?

The qualitative version of the "consider the whole" strategy is more effective in responding to this challenge. It is not concerned with the relative quantities of good and evil things. Rather, the broadening of perspective demanded is either a kind of utilitarian or aesthetic appreciation of the contribution that evils make to the overall goodness of the world, or an acknowledgment of the qualitative (and not merely quantitative) insignificance of the evils that plague human beings. Like Leibniz's theodicy five-hundred years later, which points to the necessary role that various evils play in making this the best of all possible worlds, Maimonides asks us to look more broadly at the universe as the overall context in which human sin and suffering occur. What we will then see is the "wisdom manifested in that which exists" and "the excellence and the true reality of the whole," including the contribution that the alleged evils make to it (*Guide* III.12; Maimonides 1963: II.446). In a utilitarian reading, the evils make the good things possible either by providing the necessary conditions for their occurrence or by actively bringing them about. Thus, there cannot be atonement and forgiveness without sin. Or, considered aesthetically, the evils do for the overall goodness and beauty of creation what dissonances do in a harmonious piece of music, or what shadows do for a painting done in chiaroscuro by allowing other features to stand out.

(Leibniz, who was familiar with Maimonides' *Guide*, will make a particularly nice use of this latter analogy. To anyone who, moved by the observation that "the very worst things happen to the best," doubts the metaphysical and moral perfection of the world, Leibniz remarks that

> If we look at a very beautiful picture but cover up all of it but a tiny spot, what more will appear in it, no matter how closely we study it, indeed, all

the more, the more closely we examine it, than a confused mixture of colors without beauty and without art. Yet when the covering is removed and the whole painting is viewed from a position that suits it, we come to understand that what seemed to be a thoughtless smear on the canvas has really been done with the highest artistry by the creator of the work. And what the eyes experience in painting is experienced by the ears in music. Great composers very often mix dissonances with harmonious chords to stimulate the hearer and to sting him, as it were, so that he becomes concerned about the outcome and is all the more pleased when everything is restored to order.[5])

Moreover, Maimonides adds, when one moves beyond the narrow confines of human needs and desires and expands one's vision to take in the spheres of the heavens and the separate intellects related to them, one will recognize that not everything exists for our own sake. "Man and nothing else is the most perfect and the most noble thing that has been generated from this inferior matter; but if his being is compared to that of the spheres and all the more to that of the separate beings, it is very, very contemptible" (*Guide* III.13; Maimonides 1963: II.455). Thus, just because something is evil or inconvenient for a human being, or even for human beings generally, and regardless of how often it occurs, it does not follow that it holds any great significance for the overall qualitative evaluation of the world. Dropping the anthropocentric perspective will relieve us of the urge to complain that God's creation is evil, and will do so without the problematic numbers game generated by the quantitative version of the "consider the whole" strategy.[6] Even the query as to why any evil exists at all – for which the quantitative version had no adequate answer – finds a response in this theodicean strategy.

Still, even this approach, as philosophically effective as it may be, does, in its abstraction, leave one very important question unanswered – in fact, the central question of the problem of evil that makes it matter so much to us: Why do virtuous people sometimes suffer and why do wicked people seem so often to prosper? In order to be satisfied that such phenomena are compatible with divine justice, one wants to know more

---

[5] "On the Ultimate Origination of Things" (1697); Leibniz 1976: 489–90. On Leibniz's familiarity with Maimonides, see Nadler 2019.
[6] It does so, as well, apparently without dismissing the evils that plague humans as illusory and not really evil, at least for us.

than simply that such things do not really happen very often, that they are relatively insignificant in the cosmic scheme of things, or that they make some vague and unspecified contribution to the overall goodness of the universe. Even if God is not the cause of such evils, why does he allow them at all? It is in replying to these specific questions around the relationship between virtue and flourishing that Maimonides finally appeals directly to the nature and mechanics of divine providence.[7]

Virtues

Before considering Maimonides' views on providence, and thus his more fundamental solution to the problem of why bad things happen to good people and good things to bad people, we first need to know what it is to be a good person and to lead a good life. What is, in fact, the *summum bonum*, the highest good, for a human being? What is the proper way to live? Because Maimonides, as a rabbi, adapted Aristotle's moral philosophy to his own religious purposes – as did many medieval thinkers, Jewish, Christian or Muslim – a brief excursion into Aristotelian virtue ethics will be useful before addressing the ways in which Maimonides answers these questions.

According to Aristotle's teleological view of the world, everything – whether it is a work of nature or a work of artisanship – has a proper function. Scissors, pens, even trees, and horses have their own distinct purposes: scissors cut, pens write, and horses run. Each of the different parts of the human body also has its function: eyes are for seeing, legs are for walking and running, ears are for hearing, and so on. But, Aristotle asks, what about the human being as a whole? Is there such a thing as the human function? "As eye, hand, foot and in general each of the parts evidently has a function, may one lay it down that the human being similarly has a function apart from all these? What, then, can this be?" He rules out mere living, since this is common to all things that are alive, animal and vegetable. Nor can it be appetite and perception, since these also belongs to nonhuman animals, and the human being's proper function must be "peculiar to the human being." He concludes that

---

[7] For a general discussion of Maimonides on providence, see Touati 1990. See also Reines 1972; Nuriel 1980; Raffel 1987; and Nehorai 1988.

the function uniquely characteristic of the human being is "an active life of the element that has a rational principle," "an activity of the soul in accordance with the rational principle."[8] What human beings do that makes them human is they can exercise reason, and they do so both with respect to action (through deliberation and choice) and with respect to speculation and knowing.

Now a scissors can cut well or it can cut poorly, and eyes can see well or see poorly. Similarly, human beings can perform their rational activity excellently or they can perform it poorly. The term that Aristotle uses for "excellence" is *areté*, which is also often translated as "virtue." "The human good," he concludes, "turns out to be the activity of the soul in conformity with excellence." Just as a virtuous or excellent scissors cuts well, a good or virtuous person exercises her rational faculties with excellence. In the practical domain, a virtuous person reasons well when it comes to deliberating over courses of action and making the right choices. She also reasons well with respect to theoretical matters; she is good at logical thinking and arriving at knowledge. By contrast, a vicious or bad person reasons in a deficient manner; they fall short when it comes to doing the right thing or drawing the appropriate conclusion.

> Every excellence both brings into good condition the thing of which it is the excellence and makes the work of that thing be done well. For example, the excellence of the eye makes both the eye and its work good; for it is by the excellence of the eye that we see well. Similarly, the excellence of the horse makes a horse both good in itself and good at running and carrying its rider and at awaiting the attack of the enemy. Therefore ... the excellence of a human being also will be the state which makes a human being good and which makes him do his own work well.[9]

Virtue, then, is the condition or state of a thing that allows or causes that thing to perform the proper function of its kind with excellence. In human beings we might say it is a state of character in a person, one that makes that individual function well and be a good human being.

When it comes to actions performed by human beings, what virtue does is lead them to do the right thing. Aristotle defines the right thing generally (but not always) as the mean course between extremes. He notes that "in everything that is continuous and divisible it is possible to

---

[8] *Nicomachean Ethics* 1097b21–1098a9.   [9] *Nicomachean Ethics* 1106a14–23.

take more, less, or an equal amount, and that either in terms of the thing itself or relative to us; and the equal is a mean between excess and deficiency ... Similarly, with regard to actions there is also excess, deficiency, and the mean."[10] One may eat too much for one's health, or not enough; one might, in a fit of generosity, give away too much of one's resources for one's own good, or one might be overly stingy (in view of one's wealth) and not give enough for the good of the other. Both excess and deficiency are "a form of failure," whereas acting according to the mean "is praised and a form of success." Virtue or excellence, then, "is a kind of mean, since it aims at what is intermediate." The virtuous person deliberates well over ends to be achieved and courses of action and makes the right choice by avoiding both excess and deficiency. Thus, charity is a virtue, and the charitable person gives, relative to his or her means, the right amount to those in need – she neither is stingy nor impoverishes herself with her generosity. Likewise, courage is a virtue, and the courageous person does not thoughtlessly rush headlong into danger that he cannot possibly handle, but neither is he always too afraid to tackle the challenge; the courageous person knows what his capacities are and how well prepared he is to face the threatening situation.

This doctrine of the mean applies, as well, to states of mind. There are excesses and "intermediate" conditions with respect to feelings and passions. The virtuous person not only does the right thing on the right occasion but thinks and feels what is appropriate. A good-tempered person does not get inordinately angry on the slightest provocation, but neither is he cold and insensitive. He avoids the excesses of irascibility and unfeeling and is given to anger when and how much is appropriate. The virtuous person also has the right attitude toward honors – Aristotle calls this "proper pride" – and avoids the excesses of vanity (where one is overly proud) and undue humility (where one undervalues oneself). "Moral excellence is a mean, then, between two vices, the one involving excess and the other deficiency, and it is such because its character is to aim at what is intermediate in actions and in passions."[11]

These excellences in action and feeling are moral virtues. Aristotle, however, recognized another kind of virtue or excellence pertaining to

---

[10] *Nicomachean Ethics* 1106a25–1106b24.   [11] *Nicomachean Ethics* 1109a20–24.

the intellect. If the moral virtues are virtues of character and action and develop through practice and habit, the intellectual virtues are virtues of thought and arise in a person through teaching.[12] (He is quite clear that no one is virtuous "by nature" – no one is born virtuous.) Some examples of intellectual excellence are skill in the pursuit of theoretical knowledge and wit or quickness of mind. Moral virtues and intellectual virtues are both important in a good life and make an essential contribution to living well. Each is a kind of wisdom. However, it is unclear whether Aristotle regards them as being of equal value. Does true and supreme happiness lie in the exercise of the moral virtues or the attainment of the intellectual virtues? Is the good life for a human being the practical life or the contemplative life? This is a dilemma that Maimonides himself faced.

On Being Good

As we have seen in Maimonides' letter from 1191 to Joseph ben Judah, his former student and the addressee of the *Guide of the Perplexed*, the philosopher rues how little time he has for study, what with the daily demands of his work as rabbi, physician, and communal leader.

> I tell you that I have become known as a physician among the mighty, such as the chief judge, the emirs, and the house of al-Fadil and the other princes of the land, those who lack nothing. But as for the masses, I am beyond their reach, and they have no way to approach me. And this causes me to spend the entire day in Cairo, tending to the sick, and when I get back to Fustat, all I can do for the rest of the day and into the night is to examine the medical texts that I need to consult ... As a result, I do not have a moment to study Torah except on the Sabbath, and as for other sciences, I do not have a moment to study any of them, and this harms me greatly.[13]

Maimonides is torn between two competing values, two different ways of living meaningfully. On the one hand, there is the life of practical activity; on the other hand, the life of contemplation. He cherishes the latter, but recognizes the importance of the former.

---

[12] *Nicomachean Ethics* 1103a14–19. [13] Quoted in Halbertal 2014: 63–64.

This same tension that Maimonides experienced existentially in his daily routine also finds expression in his philosophical writings, particularly when he turns to goodness and the *summum bonum* of human life. He insists in the final chapter of the *Guide* that "the true human perfection ... consists in the acquisition of the rational virtues – I refer to the conception of intelligibles, which teach true opinions concerning the divine things." He says that this intellectual knowledge "is in true reality the ultimate end; this is what gives the individual true perfection, a perfection belonging to him alone" (*Guide* III.54; Maimonides 1963: II.635). Maimonides notes that the person who has reached perfection of the intellect and "apprehended the true realities" achieves a state in which his mind is singularly focused on these higher truths while, with his body, he only goes through the motions as he interacts with the world around him; he "talks with people and is occupied with his bodily necessities while his intellect is wholly turned towards God" (*Guide* III.51; Maimonides 1963: II.623). Such "excellent men begrudge the times in which they are turned away from Him by other occupations" (II.622).

And yet, in those same final chapters Maimonides suggests that this occupation, even obsession with the intelligibles, and in particular the apprehension of God, is not in fact the ultimate human end, that the activity of pure contemplation and the perfection of the intellect does not by itself constitute true human perfection. Rather, the final goal is subsequent to such contemplation, namely, putting what has been studied into action and working to improve the lives of others.

This apparent conflict – even inconsistency – in Maimonides' thought has long perplexed his readers. It is the same problem that, as I have mentioned, arises in Aristotle's ethical writings. Does the highest human excellence and perfection for Maimonides consist in *theoria* or *praxis*? Is the *summum bonum* to be found in the life of contemplation itself, in the exercise of the intellectual virtues, or in the life of action informed by such intellectual knowledge and the practice of moral virtues? In short: What is it to be a truly good person? How should we live?

Maimonides' account of the moral virtues is unmistakably Aristotelian.[14] In his introduction to his commentary on the *Mishnah*

---

[14] For a study of Maimonides' ethics, see Weiss 1991.

tractate *Pirké Avot* (Ethics of the Fathers) – the essay is commonly referred to as "Eight Chapters" – Maimonides explains that the virtues are "psychic conditions and dispositions" in the soul which are "midway between two reprehensible extremes, one of which is characterized by an exaggeration, the other by a deficiency. Good deeds are the product of these dispositions." He offers as an example the virtue that governs our behaviors dealing with pleasure.

> Abstemiousness is a disposition which adopts a mid-course between inordinate passion and total insensibility to pleasure. Abstemiousness, then, is a proper rule of conduct, and the psychic disposition which gives rise to it is an ethical quality; but inordinate passion, the extreme of excess, and total insensibility to enjoyment, the extreme of deficiency, are both absolutely pernicious. The psychic dispositions from which these two extremes, inordinate passion and insensibility, result – the one being an exaggeration, the other a deficiency – are alike classed among moral imperfections.

Likewise, he defines liberality or charity as "a mean between miserliness and extravagance," courage as "a mean between recklessness and cowardice," and humility as a mean between "arrogance and self-abasement" ("Eight Chapters," IV; Maimonides 1972: 367–8).

A more detailed presentation of Maimonides' ethical theory appears in the *Mishneh Torah*, especially *Hilkhot Deot* (Laws of Human Dispositions). While we are all endowed with various character traits, each individual tends to be governed by a particular state.

> One type of man is wrathful; he is constantly angry. There is the calm individual, who is never moved to anger, or, if at all, he will be slightly angry, during a period of several years. There is the prideful man and the one who is exceptionally humble. There is the man ruled by his appetites – he will never be satisfied from pursuing his desires; and there is the very pure of heart, who does not desire even the little that the body needs. The greedy man cannot be satisfied with all the money in the world ... and the man who puts a check on himself, he is satisfied with even a little, which is not enough for his needs, and he does not bother to pursue and attain what he lacks. (*Mishneh Torah, Hilkhot Deot* I.1)

These extremes of character are vices. Maimonides warns that they "do not reflect a proper path," and that one should not allow oneself to be governed by them in one's behavior. Rather, if we should find ourselves tending toward one extreme or another, we should seek "correction" and get ourselves "back to what is proper and walk in the path of the good." This "straight path" is found among the "intermediate points," and these intermediates or means – "equidistant from either of the extremes" – represent the virtues. So, rather than being either foolhardy or cowardly, one should engage danger only when it is a serious matter and one has the resources to deal with it; and rather than being profligate and "spreading money about" or being stingy, one should give charitably according to one's means. In terms of states of mind, the middle course to being overly cheerful ("with excessive laughing") or sad and depressed is to be "quietly happy at all times, with a friendly countenance" (*Mishneh Torah, Hilkhot Deot* I.5).

At this point, one might reasonably ask: If a person is given to one of the extremes, how exactly is she supposed to get herself on the straight path? In both of these halakhic works, Maimonides' answer is the same: practice!

> These moral excellences or defects cannot be acquired or implanted in the soul except by means of the frequent repetition of acts resulting from these qualities, which, practiced during a long period of time, accustoms us to them. If these acts performed are good ones, then we shall have gained a virtue; but if they are bad, we shall have acquired a vice. ("Eight Chapters," IV; Maimonides 1972: 369)

The process for becoming virtuous, presented by Aristotle and seconded by Maimonides, is that, first, you either find a virtuous person on whom to model your behavior or figure out for yourself what the mean is between any two extremes; then, you do the things that the virtuous person does, act like a virtuous person, and follow the mean. In the beginning, of course, it is all an act – because you are not yet virtuous, you are not doing the virtuous things *as* a virtuous person does them, naturally and instinctively; you are merely imitating a virtuous person. However, over time, as you become habituated to acting in virtuous ways, you also begin to develop the inner condition of the virtuous person – their motivations, desires, and feelings.

> How can one train himself to follow these temperaments to the extent that they become a permanent fixture of his personality? He should perform – repeat – and perform a third time – the acts which conform

to the standards of the middle road temperaments. He should do this constantly, until these acts are easy for him and do not present any difficulty. Then, these temperaments will become a fixed part of his personality. (*Mishneh Torah, Hilkhot Deot*, I.7)

A possible rule of thumb for changing one's character and moving toward the mean is to overcompensate a bit. If one is overly cowardly, then for a while one should engage impulsively with danger, so as eventually to land in the comfortable middle. If one is excessively stingy, then start giving away more than you should so as to accommodate yourself to what is proper.

> We tell a wrathful man to train himself to feel no reaction even if he is beaten or cursed. He should follow this course of behavior for a long time, until the anger is uprooted from his heart. The man who is full of pride should cause himself to experience much disgrace ... One should take a similar course with each of the other traits. A person who swayed in the direction of one of the extremes should move in the direction of the opposite extreme and accustom himself to that for a long time, until he has returned to the proper path, which is the midpoint for each and every temperament. (*Mishneh Torah, Hilkhot Deot*, II.2)

A person can correct any deviation from the mean in one direction by going toward – but not all the way to – the other extreme and thereby establish a balance.

There are some exceptions to these general rules. For certain traits of character there is no middle way. These are temperaments to be avoided altogether. Among these are arrogance, which is never good, not even in moderation, and anger ("an exceptionally bad quality" which is to be avoided in any degree – here Maimonides departs from Aristotle, who, as we saw, allows that it is proper to get angry in the right circumstances). Similarly, hatred, envy, and jealousy, no matter in what degree, are all vices, never virtues.

There is a social dimension to the acquisition of the moral virtues. One is more likely to find virtuous people to imitate, as well as people who will actively encourage one in the practice of the virtues, if one lives among virtuous people.

> It is natural for a man's character and actions to be influenced by his friends and associates and for him to follow the local norms of behavior.

> Therefore, he should associate with the righteous and be constantly in the company of the wise, so as to learn from their deeds. Conversely, he should keep away from the wicked who walk in darkness, so as not to learn from their deeds . . . A person who lives in a place where the norms of behavior are evil and the inhabitants do not follow the straight path should move to a place where the people are righteous and follow the ways of the good. (*Mishneh Torah, Hilkhot Deot* VI.1)

The social aspects of moral development have clear political implications. It would seem to be incumbent upon the leaders of any polity to craft laws that encourage, even reward virtuous behavior and punish vicious actions. Lawmakers, in other words, have a duty – to the well-being of their citizens and to the security and flourishing of their community – to do what they can to mold people into virtuous characters. They are to act so as to ensure the conditions for cooperation and mutual aid and a strong educational system that inculcates in citizens a proper conception of what is good and right.

Maimonides calls the virtuous person whose actions are habitually set on the mean – whose character traits are "intermediate and equally balanced" – "a wise person [*hakham*]." This is the ideal for most people, and well within their reach. "Ought" implies "can" here, and there is nothing that Maimonides is urging that, under ordinary circumstances, is impossible. There are some individuals, however, who have chosen to go a bit further and lean into one of the extremes, typically in the direction of the deficiency of the trait in question. Such an individual is "pious [*hasid*]." As long as she does not deviate too far toward the extreme, her character and supererogatory behavior remain within the realm of virtue.

> A person who carefully examines his behavior and therefore deviates slightly from the mean to either side is called pious. One who shuns pride and turns to the other extreme and carries himself lowly is called pious. This is the quality of piety. However, if he separates himself from pride only to the extent that he reaches the mean and displays humility, he is called wise. This is the quality of wisdom. (*Mishneh Torah, Hilkhot Deot* I.5)

If the wise person charitably gives in such way that she finds a balance between what is needed and what she can reasonably afford, the pious person will go beyond and give even more, yet not so much as to thoroughly impoverish herself.

The *Summum Bonum*

In his halakhic works, Maimonides suggests that the attainment of the moral virtues – those states of character that determine one to think, act, and feel according to the mean – is our highest good and our most perfect condition. "If a man will always carefully discriminate as regards his actions, directing them to the medium course, he will reach the highest degree of perfection possible to a human being, thereby approaching God and sharing in His happiness" ("Eight Chapters," V; Maimonides 1972: 376).

Perhaps this is, indeed, the best that most people can hope for: to reach the condition of the *wise* person (though it certainly will not be an easy thing to do). In our ordinary lives, with all the obligations, demands, and constraints with which we find ourselves – from family, friends, work, physical abilities, financial resources, etc. – we may still strive to be as ethical as possible and to do those things that appear, in our better judgment, to be in the best interest of others and not too contrary to our own interests. We will aid the poor by giving to charity, jump in the water to save someone who is drowning, and generally act in benevolent and considerate ways toward our fellow human beings. We cannot be moral saints, and perhaps such ethical purity, where sanctity can descend into sanctimoniousness, is not even desirable.[15] But we, the multitude, can, and should, strive at least for a life of moral virtue.

However, Maimonides' discussion of human perfection in the *Guide*, where his target audience is on a higher philosophical plane, leaves no doubt as to where the moral virtues stand in the grander scheme of things. Without the moral virtues of character, one cannot possibly achieve human perfection and the highest happiness. But Maimonides is as clear as can be that as valuable as moral virtue is, it is not itself our ultimate good, our *summum bonum*.

Perfection or flourishing arrives in discrete stages for Maimonides (*Guide* I.34). It begins with what he calls "the perfection of possessions."

---

[15] On this see Wolf 1982.

This is a purely relational condition involving external goods, whereby an individual possesses the necessities for life, even for a comfortable life. Without the satisfaction of the most basic needs, such as shelter, food, financial means, and friends, one will have little time or concern for the right way of living, much less hope of truly flourishing and leading the best kind of life for a human being.

The second "species" of perfection is an intrinsic one – not a matter of relation to other things – and has "a greater connection than the first with the individual's self. It concerns the perfection of the bodily constitution and shape." Speaking in his capacity as a physician, Maimonides notes that an individual should enjoy a harmonious temperament, his body should be "well-proportioned" and strong, and he should be generally physically healthy. Like the lack of basic necessities, illness, or disability – and here we would have to supplement Maimonides' emphasis on the body with a concern for mental health – will distract one from the pursuit of higher goods such as virtue and wisdom. Without a sound body and a sound mind, one cannot reach the next stage of human perfection.

The third, "greater" level of perfection concerns not the individual's body but his "self." This is where the moral virtues come in. Maimonides insists that "preparatory moral training should be carried out ... so that man should be in a state of extreme uprightness and perfection" (*Guide* I.34; Maimonides 1963: I.77). This kind of perfection "consists in the individual's moral habits having attained their ultimate excellence." The morally perfected individual has those states of character that are the virtues and that direct him to seek the mean in all that he does. He is, in other words, *hakham*. Maimonides notes, further, that most of the commandments of the Torah "serve no other end than the attainment of this species of perfection" and the inculcation of the moral virtues (*Guide* III.54; Maimonides 1963: II.634–5). The actions they direct us to do are just how a virtuous person following the mean would behave, and the actions they forbid are the extreme things that a virtuous person would never do.

Maimonides insists, however, that the moral virtues, while they (unlike the perfection of possessions) "subsist in the individual's self," are of only instrumental or social value. "For all moral habits are concerned with what occurs between a human individual and someone else." Generosity, courage, and the other Aristotelian virtues conceived as means between extremes and that Maimonides discusses in the ethical texts of the *Mishneh Torah* and the *Commentary on the Mishnah* are of no use, and thus of no value, for a person who is not engaged in interpersonal relationships. "For if you suppose a human individual is alone, acting on no one, you will find that all his moral virtues are in vain and without employment and unneeded, and that they do not perfect the individual in anything." Maimonides concludes that "this species of perfection is ... a preparation for something else and not an end in itself" (*Guide* III.54; Maimonides 1963: II.635).

But what precisely are the moral virtues a preparation for? What can be more important than living well in the world, including treating others in the altruistic and beneficial ways that we ordinarily regard as "ethical?" Maimonides' answer is perhaps what might be expected of a philosopher. Excellence of moral character, he claims, is only a necessary but not sufficient condition, only a preparation, for some higher, more perfect human achievement – namely, rational virtue or the perfection of the intellect by way of metaphysical, theological, and cosmological knowledge, especially as found among philosophers and prophets.

> The fourth species [of perfection] is the true human perfection; it consists in the acquisition of the rational virtues – I refer to the conception of intelligibles, which teach true opinions concerning the divine things. This is in true reality the ultimate end; this is what gives the individual true perfection, a perfection belonging to him alone; and it gives him permanent perdurance; through it man is man. (*Guide* III.54; Maimonides 1963: II.635)

Knowledge is the supreme good, the highest purpose of the Law, and the immediate bond between human beings and God. Through the acquisition of true speculative opinions about the cosmos and about God – what Maimonides calls "natural science" and "divine science," respectively – a human being attains the ultimate perfection. It is a purely intellectual kind of wisdom (*hokhmah*), distinct from the practical wisdom (what Aristotle called *phronesis*) that guides us daily through the world. This theoretical wisdom is, moreover, accompanied by the affective states of joy (in its possession) and love (of its object). "Love is proportionate to apprehension," Maimonides insists, and he makes it clear that he is referring to the abstract intellectual apprehension of necessary and eternal truths and not merely sensory or imaginative perception of ephemeral, mundane, and physically beautiful things.

Maimonides has God describe this epistemic goal in the following terms: "One should glory in the apprehension of Myself and in the knowledge of My attributes." But recall that the knowledge of God's essence in itself is beyond our reach, and God does not literally have any attributes for us to grasp. What is in play here is, as we have seen, a knowledge of God's "actions" as these are extrapolated from the world, from the order and nature of things, including the laws that govern both this sublunar realm and the heavens above. It thus includes the natural sciences (especially physics and astronomy), metaphysics (the study of being and essences), and theology (the knowledge of God). The wise person understands the structure and dynamics of the cosmos, as a twelfth-century thinker like Maimonides conceives these: How the planets are embedded in crystalline spheres that carry them around the earth, with the stars fixed in their own sphere beyond those of the planets; how these spheres are ensouled and how their rotating motions are caused jointly by friction, as the outermost sphere of the universe rotates and generates the motions of the inner, concentric spheres, and by the desire in each sphere's soul to imitate (with perfect circular motion) the "separate intellect" (or angel) associated with it. Because the mind of this individual, who is a philosopher, is well prepared to receive the "overflow" of knowledge that descends from God through the separate intellects to the Agent Intellect that oversees the sublunar realm, he can tap into that knowledge and transform his own potential intellect into an actual or "acquired" intellect that is filled with that knowledge. He thereby possesses the Creator's knowledge of his creation.

Now all this seems very Aristotelian and very medieval, and thus quite foreign to how we think today about the acquisition of scientific knowledge, cosmology, and other epistemological and metaphysical matters. But the general and essential point that Maimonides is making here – a lesson that can be found in philosophical traditions from antiquity to the modern era, from Plato to Spinoza to certain contemporary versions of eudaimonist ethics – is that the life of the mind, whereby one becomes knowledgeable in a deep, intellectual way about the nature of things and arrives at an understanding of oneself and of nature, represents true human flourishing. One is simply better off as a human being – extraordinarily better off – in a life devoted to the pursuit of truth. This, Maimonides would say, is not merely his opinion but an objective matter of fact grounded in human nature.

The Practical Life and the Contemplative Life

We are still left with the question as to the value of the moral virtues. Are they meant only to prepare us for attaining some final goal, a purely intellectual condition that, as some scholars have argued, is, on Maimonides' account, extremely difficult if not impossible for embodied human beings to attain?[16] Or is our ultimate objective one step further, namely, putting that intellectual perfection to work in a life of action that is a kind of practical *imitatio Dei*?[17]

It is tempting to conclude from the final chapters of the *Guide* that for Maimonides the true human perfection is indeed the intellectual variety alone, and that acts of loving-kindness, justice, and righteousness that constitute the *imitatio Dei* are supererogatory consequences or by-products of this perfection. He tells us that

> Those who set their thought to work after having attained perfection in the divine science turn wholly toward God, may He be cherished and held sublime, renounce what is other than He, and direct all the acts of their intellect toward an examination of the beings with a view to drawing from them proof with regard to Him, so as to know His governance of them in whatever way it is possible.

He adds that "after apprehension, total devotion to [God] and the employment of intellectual thought in constantly loving [God] should be aimed at" (*Guide* III.51; Maimonides 1963: II.620–1). The person who has achieved this superb condition will resist any attempt to draw

---

[16] Stern 2013. For a contrasting view, see Lasker 2010.
[17] This question has generated a good deal of scholarly debate. Those who read Maimonides as claiming that human perfection consists in intellectual perfection include Altman 1972, Kreisel 1989, Blumenthal 1981, and Stern 2013. Those who opt for what Menachem Kellner calls "practical perfection" include Hartman 1976 (especially chapter 5) and Kellner 1990. Pines (1979) argues that true human perfection is practical, political, or moral, not because it follows intellectual perfection but because the latter is impossible. Stern agrees with Pines that for Maimonides intellectual perfection is not humanly realizable, but he insists that it remains the human ideal. See also Manekin 2005: 90–92.

him away from his contemplative state and resent any time he must spend engaged in the messy affairs of the world.

At the same time, Maimonides notes, as mentioned above, that even the person who apprehends God and his ways through a rational contemplation of intelligible truths will feel compelled to engage in practical activity among his fellow human beings that is an expression of what has been learned of God's nature – whatever little can be known of it in a metaphorical way, through the projection of human agency and characteristics – and God's "actions" in the cosmos. Maimonides says that "those actions [of God] that ought to be known and imitated are loving-kindness, justice, and righteousness." (In this respect, Maimonides' intellectually perfected individual is like the philosopher in Plato's metaphorical story of the cave in the *Republic*. Liberated from the shadow play in the cave to find enlightenment in the vision of the true realities, he is motivated, even duty-bound, to go back down into the cave to bring others up from their enslavement to illusions.)

Maimonides thus says that God has made it clear that "it is My purpose that there should come from you loving-kindness, righteousness, and judgment in the earth," that we should assimilate God's attributes as we apprehend them through our study of nature and Torah. We should be gracious and merciful and "walk in his ways" in our own actions, and "this should be our way of life" (*Guide* III.54; Maimonides 1963: II.637). Thus, Maimonides concludes, "the utmost virtue of man is to become like unto Him, may He be exalted, as far as he is able; which means that we should make our actions like unto His" (*Guide* I.54; Maimonides 1963: I.128; see also *Mishneh Torah, Hilkhot Deot*, I.5–6). The highest virtue does not involve a withdrawal from the world but an active moral engagement within it. Having secured the highest good for himself, the virtuous person then works knowledgeably to secure it for others.

Here, too, I believe, Maimonides recognizes something that will reappear in various forms in later moral philosophy. With the achievement of the highest intellectual knowledge, the virtuous person is now even better equipped to exercise the moral virtues that initially served to prepare him for that superb condition. Which is to say, there are important differences between three distinct kinds of moral agent, even when they all act virtuously. First, there is the person whose actions just happen to be in accordance with what virtue demands, despite the fact that his motives are far from virtuous. Immanuel Kant, in his ethical writings, gives the example of a prudent shopkeeper who does not cheat his customers – not because it is the right thing to do but because it would be bad for business.[18] Then there is the person whose moral behavior is the result of habit. Having been conditioned, through practice, to finding the mean, she does the right thing because it now comes naturally to her. Finally, there is the truly wise person whose moral behavior as he returns to the world from his contemplative retreat is the result of intellectual perfection and the study of God's ways. The first person is hardly deserving of praise for his actions, given his self-serving motive. The second person, acting and feeling from an acquired disposition of character, is undoubtedly a good person and morally admirable. Best of all, however, is the person who not only naturally and unfailingly does what is right but also knows *why* it is right, and that is why they do it. It would seem that only the intellectually gifted – in Maimonides' terms, the philosopher and the prophet – are at this highest level of moral goodness. In this respect, I must disagree with Julius Guttmann's assessment that in Maimonides' system morality loses its primacy, moves "to the periphery," and becomes "only a means to the theoretical or contemplative purpose of religion."[19] What Maimonides does, in fact, is elevate the moral life and, at least for the wise person, put it on a more secure, because less subjective, foundation.

The more we know – about the universe, nature, and ourselves – the more we have achieved intellectually, the more perfect we are. This perfection has important, even life-enhancing benefits. It puts one under the protection of divine providence, albeit a divine providence that, in keeping with Maimonides' rejection of any kind of anthropomorphic conception of God, is to be understood in remarkably naturalistic rather than superstitious terms. And with providence, along with our understanding of what it is to be a good person, we finally return to the theodicean problem with which we started: Why do bad things happen to good people?

---

[18] See *Groundwork for the Metaphysics of Morals*, Chapter 1.   [19] Guttmann 1964: 182.

Divine Providence

In Maimonides' account of divine providence, God does not really *do* anything. In fact, it is a kind of providence that, with some minor adjustments, does not require a belief in God at all. Even Spinoza could – and, I believe, does – accept its basic elements.

Maimonides begins his discussion of providence by rejecting four different views on the topic.[20] The Epicurean view is that there is no providence at all, and that everything happens as a result of the random permutations of matter. This, for Maimonides, is a nonstarter, since it is inconsistent with demonstrated metaphysical and theological principles; it is not really a theory of providence at all. The orthodox Aristotelian view is that divine governance extends only to the everlasting and immutable elements of the cosmos. The celestial spheres and their contents, as well as the species of things, are provided by God with what is necessary for their preservation. Individual existents in this sublunar realm, however, are watched over by providence only to the extent that they are endowed with essential attributes determined by the species to which they belong. Thus, as any individual horse will naturally have certain characteristic properties and behaviors just because it is a horse, so a human being is ordinarily possessed of reason, a sense of humor, and a variety of emotions and instincts, all of which aid his preservation, by virtue of belonging to the species "human being." Everything else that happens to a horse or a human being that does not flow from its species characteristics, however – everything, that is, that does not belong to it essentially and by virtue of its horse-nature or human-nature – is due to chance. While Maimonides for the most part rejects the Aristotelian view, mainly because it distances God too much from the governance of things, he believes that there is indeed an element of truth to it, one that he will incorporate in his own account.

The third account Maimonides rejects is the theory of providence offered by the Ash'arite school of Muslim theologians, according to which *nothing* in the universe is due to chance. Rather, everything is

---

[20] He actually considers five views before presenting what he calls his own. But it has been argued by many commentators that Maimonides' view is substantially identical with the fifth view – "the opinion of our law," the view of Torah – and constitutes only a more sophisticated, philosophical understanding of it; see Touati 1990: 149–50.

brought about directly through the will of God. Providence thus extends to every aspect of every event in nature, from the punishment of a sinner to the falling of a leaf from a tree. Maimonides insists that this account is unacceptable because it renders divine law useless. If God does everything, then no human being would have the freedom to do or refrain from doing what the law commands or proscribes. Thus, for the sake of glorifying divine power it makes a mockery of divine justice.

The fourth opinion also states that divine providence watches over everything, but adds that human beings are free in their actions. Moreover, God is responsible for distributing rewards and punishments to all beings – not just humans – not by sheer acts of will (as the Ash'arite view implies) but through wisdom and justice. Maimonides objects to this view on the ground that it is absurd to extend divine justice beyond the realm of human agency. Just as the partisans of this view say that when a blameless person suffers, divine justice will provide him with a greater reward in the world-to-come, so they must say that when a particular animal is killed by another it was better for it to be so and it will receive a recompense in the hereafter. "They say in the same way that if this mouse, which has not sinned, is devoured by a cat or a hawk, His wisdom has required this with regard to the mouse and that the latter will receive compensation in the other world for what has happened to it" (*Guide* III.17; Maimonides 1963: II.468). To Maimonides, such an idea is "disgraceful."

Maimonides' own view is that in our sublunar world the only individuals to whom God's providence extends are human beings. For all other creatures, providence covers only the species and their preservation; everything else is left to chance (as the Aristotelian view claims). Moreover, *all* of the events and activities of a human life, without exception, are a matter of divine justice and therefore fall under providence.

> I for one believe that in this lowly world ... divine providence watches only over the individuals belonging to the human species and that in this species alone all the circumstances of the individuals and the good and evil that befall them are consequent upon the deserts, just as it says: "For all his ways are judgment." (*Guide* III.17; Maimonides 1963: II.471)

Thus, if a ship at sea is sunk by a storm or a hard wind blows a house down, this is due to "pure chance" – or, more properly, the regular but (from the perspective of human expectations) unforeseen and uncontrollable causal order of nature – no less than the fact that a particular leaf has fallen off a tree at a one moment rather than another. But that certain people had (freely) gone on board the ship that sunk or had been sitting in the house that was blown down is due not to chance but to "divine will in accordance with the deserts of those people as determined in His judgments" (*Guide* III.17; Maimonides 1963: II.472). On the face of it, this seems callous and cruel. What does Maimonides have in mind?

Now one possible, even natural, way of conceiving the divine *modus operandi* in providence for Maimonides needs to be ruled out from the start. There are passages in which Maimonides speaks as if God, seeing the virtues and vices of particular human beings, actively and intentionally chooses to reward and punish them as individuals – perhaps in just the vulgar way that one might think of providence, with God bringing disaster upon one person while snatching another person from the jaws of death (much as Daniel is saved in the lions' den). Thus, just as Maimonides insists that the people are on board the ship because of the "divine will in accordance with the deserts of those people as determined in His judgments," so he elsewhere notes how the fate met by many people is "due not to neglect and the withdrawal of providence, but was a punishment for those men because they deserved what befell them" (*Guide* III.17; Maimonides 1963: II.473). But it is clear that this anthropomorphic model of divine action, with God willfully intervening to save or punish a person as if through a miracle, is inconsistent with what we have seen Maimonides considers the proper conception of God; and such language may be only an instance of Maimonides' practice of adapting his writing to conceal from the philosophically unsophisticated unprepared reader the truth of the matter.

In fact, God's role in providence is, so to speak, much more passive. There is a divinely established system in place that is there for individual human beings to take advantage of or not, as they choose. And it is the virtuous – understood as those who pursue intellectual virtue, and not merely moral virtue – who choose to do so, while all others are left without its protection.

Maimonides distinguishes between general providence and individual providence. General providence (what in Samuel ibn Tibbon's twelfth-century Hebrew translation, which Maimonides approved, gets rendered as *hashgahah minit*, providence of the kind) is constituted by the broadly distributed characteristics of the species, oriented to its preservation and (barring unusual circumstances) provided equally to all members of the species. Individual providence (*hashgahah 'ishit*, providence of the person) is particularized to individuals and distributed only according to merits. Both varieties of providence are understood in highly naturalistic and Aristotelian terms. While general providence covers all living things according to their kinds, individual providence comes into play only in the realm of human agency.

Individual providence, Maimonides says, is a function of the overflow of knowledge from God through the separate intellects (including, penultimately, the Agent Intellect governing this sublunar realm) to the human intellect of those who are properly prepared. To the extent that a person receives this overflow, she is under the protection of providence.

> Divine providence is consequent upon the divine overflow ... providence is consequent upon the intellect and attached to it. For providence can only come from an intelligent being, from One who is an intellect perfect with a supreme perfection, than which there is no higher. Accordingly, everyone with whom something of this overflow is united, will be reached by providence to the extent to which he is reached by the intellect. (*Guide* III.17; Maimonides 1963: II.471–2, 474)

Individual providence is not an all or nothing affair, but proportionate to the degree to which a person is truly virtuous – that is, proportionate not only to her moral character, but above all to the degree to which she has turned cognitively toward God, directed her attention to the knowledge flowing from God and thereby perfected her intellect.

> When any individual has obtained, because of the disposition of his matter and his training, a greater proportion of this overflow than others, providence will of necessity watch more carefully over him than over others – if, that is to say, providence is, as I have mentioned, consequent upon the intellect. Accordingly, divine providence does not watch in an equal manner over all the individuals of the human species, but providence is graded as their human perfection is graded. (*Guide* III.18; Maimonides 1963: II.475)

In this sense, providence is a reward for (intellectual) virtue and the perfection of our highest faculties. And despite Maimonides' claim that the suffering of many is "due not to neglect and the withdrawal of providence, but was a punishment for those men because they deserved what befell them," it seems clear that it is precisely through approach and withdrawal – that is, the *human being's* willful intellectual approaching to and withdrawing from the overflow – that providence operates. As long as a person is actively enjoying the epistemic connection to the divine overflow, she is *ipso facto* protected; providence is watching over – or, better, engaged in – her and she is guarded from vagaries of chance. On the other hand, when a person is not attending to God (either because he has never made the effort or because, having achieved the intellectual connection to the overflow, he has temporarily become distracted, perhaps by the pleasures of the senses), he is abandoned to chance and left to his own devices in the face of the slings and arrows of outrageous fortune. The person who is not embracing the overflow is not enjoying its benefits. He is at the mercy of nature's elements and his well-being is subject to whatever may or may not come his way. Providence is no longer watching over him – not because God is actively punishing him but because through his own actions he has taken himself outside of the care that providence (the overflow) offers.

> With regard to providence watching over excellent men and neglecting the ignorant, it is said: "He will keep the feet of his holy ones, but the wicked shall be put to silence in darkness; for not by strength shall man prevail." It says thereby that the fact that some individuals are preserved from calamities, whereas those befall others, is due not to their bodily forces and their natural dispositions ... but to their perfection and deficiency, I mean their nearness to or remoteness from God. For this reason, those who are near to Him are exceedingly well protected ... whereas those who are far from Him are given over to whatever may happen to befall them. For there is nothing to protect them against whatever may occur; for they are like one walking in darkness, whose destruction is assured. (*Guide* III.18; Maimonides 1963: II.475–6)

Those who do not strive for intellectual perfection have no more providential protection than nonhuman animals. They enjoy only general providence and whatever tools for survival the species confers upon them (as well as upon everyone else).

This is all very opaque, as Maimonides lays things out in his own quasi-Aristotelian, quasi-rabbinic idiom. What exactly does he have in mind here? There is some ambiguity as to just what is the nature of the protection that, according to Maimonides, divine providence provides. Commentators, from Maimonides' time onward, have been divided between two ways of reading his account.[21] On one reading, what the knowledge brought to the human intellect by the divine overflow gives to the righteous person is a way actually to escape the evils around him. At one point Maimonides says of the intellectually perfected person that "no evil at all will befall him." If he should find himself in the midst of a pitched battle, then "even if one thousand were killed to your left and ten thousand to your right, no evil at all would befall you" (*Guide* III.51; Maimonides 1963: II.626–7). This is a very extraordinary claim for Maimonides, or anyone, to make. It seems to suggest that the virtuous person can truly escape from the vicissitudes of fortune that affect all beings in this world – to become, in effect, immune to the forces of nature that govern all events and affect the well-being of all creatures and that make life a chancey thing. Can Maimonides really mean this? Will the virtuous person never be attacked by another, never fall down stairs, stub his toe, or even get a paper cut on his finger?

Some commentators have concluded that "no," he cannot really mean this. Even the virtuous person cannot completely remove the element of chance from his life. One of those arrows is bound to fall on him. He will, at some point, stub his toe or get a paper cut. Fortunately, another interpretation of Maimonides' account is possible. On this reading, the person who attends to God, while not literally escaping the evils that naturally come his way – especially the physical evils of the first kind (which affect his body) and the moral evils of the second kind (due to the sinful behavior of others), which tend to be due to circumstances well beyond one's control – will be less troubled by them. The virtuous person's mind is fixated on a true and lasting good, and he thereby grows immune to the lure of mutable goods and inured to the travails of his body. He cares less about wealth, honor, and even

---

[21] Both Samuel and Moses ibn Tibbon, for example, the translator of Maimonides's *Guide* and his son, remark upon this tension; see Diesendruck 1936. For an attempt to resolve the ambiguity, see Touati 1990.

material comforts. Like the Stoic sage, he has achieved through his own epistemic resources a lasting state of spiritual well-being, tranquility, and equanimity, and so his happiness is not dependent on external circumstances and thereby subject to the vagaries of chance.

Maimonides says that this is the condition of Job at the end of the Bible story. As Maimonides reads Job's first speech to the friends who offer him cold comfort in the midst of his horrific torments, Job adopts the Aristotelian view: God is not watching over individuals, and is causing suffering for no good reason at all, "because of his contempt for the human species and abandonment of it."[22] After God has spoken, however, Job achieves a state of understanding: "He knew God with a certain knowledge, he admitted that true happiness, which is the knowledge of the deity, is guaranteed to all who know Him and that a human being cannot be troubled in it by any of all the misfortunes in question" ("Eight Chapters," IV; Maimonides 1972: 367–8). It is not that the good person experiences no loss or harm in his life; after all, Job has suffered miserably and lost practically everything. Rather, consumed with his bond with God and possessing true (spiritual) happiness, he cares less about those losses. He may see evils in his lifetime, but they will not constitute an "affliction" for him – he does not see them as *true* evils. The lesson Maimonides sees here is both a Stoic one and a Socratic one: the harms that the world brings cannot touch us in our most important part. After all, it was Socrates who, at the end of his trial as portrayed in Plato's dialogue *Apology*, said that "nothing can harm a good person, neither in life nor in death."[23] You can hurt or even kill a good person, but you cannot touch his soul.

Now this spiritualistic reading of Maimonides' account of providence, based in part on his interpretation of the Job story, is certainly a legitimate one and easily derived from the texts. It makes good sense of much of what the *Guide* has to say about providence and evil, and it also does not have the implausible implication that a good person will never suffer harm of any sort. And yet, we should not be so quick to dismiss

---

[22] Maimonides identifies each of the speakers in the Book of Job with one of the philosophical views on providence (excepting the Epicurean view): Job = Aristotelian theory, Eliphaz = Torah theory, Bildad = Mutazilite theory, Zophar = Asharite theory, and Elihu = Maimonidean theory; see Guide III.23. For a discussion of Maimonides' reading of Job, see Eisen 2004: chapter 3.
[23] Plato, *Apology*, 41d.

altogether the first, more extreme reading. That is, I think that Maimonides does indeed believe that the virtuous person can diminish the degree to which he is at the mercy of circumstance – not entirely, perhaps, but to a very significant degree. And the virtuous person can do so not simply because he does not recognize the things brought by chance as real goods or evils but also because such a person – unlike the nonvirtuous person – can exercise some control over the events in which they engage and over the things that happen to them.

As we have seen, the overflow in which the supremely virtuous person – the intellectually perfected person – participates is a knowledge about the cosmos at large, but especially about the order of things in the world. The overflow thus carries information about nature, just the kind of understanding that allows an individual to successfully navigate his way around the obstacles to his flourishing that our environment regularly presents. Thus, a person who has refined his intellect in the proper way will not just care less about what might be lost on a ship at sea but he will also know not to get on the doomed ship in the first place (perhaps because he knows a storm is coming, or sees that the ship is either poorly constructed or badly captained). The good person will, just because of his understanding of things, excel at living, even thriving, in a world that is itself, at best, indifferent to his well-being.

We really do not need to choose between the two readings. We can say that the intellectual condition of the virtuous person does two things. First, it guides him successfully through the world with minimal harm. Second, it makes him indifferent to whatever harms or evils he does happen to encounter despite the protection provided by providence. Notice, too, that on either reading, providence does not consist in the active and willful intervention of God in human affairs; it is not that God chooses in particular to reward the person who has united herself to the overflow. This kind of agency would, once again, be inconsistent with what we have seen is Maimonides' non-anthropomorphic conception of God. Rather, quite naturalistically, the knowledge acquired by the virtuous person through the overflow affords her an advantage in the world. "The overflow of the divine intellect ... guides the actions of righteous men, and perfects the knowledge of excellent men with regard to what they know" (*Guide* III.18; Maimonides 1963: II.475).

Why Do Bad Things Happen to Good People?

This brings us back, finally, to the familiar version of the problem of evil: Why do good and innocent people suffer? Maimonides' response is that, in essence, they do not. If a person suffers misfortune, it is because he deserves it.[24] If a virtuous person suffers, it is, regardless of appearances, because he has done something that has taken him outside the protection of providence, if only for a brief moment in time. The intellectual bond to God and the overflow can be broken, by a lapse in attention or redirection of the mind to lesser things. When that happens, the knowledge it brings is no longer doing its protective work.

> The providence of God, may he be exalted, is constantly watching over those who have obtained this overflow, which is permitted to everyone who makes efforts with a view to obtaining it. If a man's thought is free from distraction, if he apprehends Him, may He be exalted, in the right way and rejoices in what he apprehends, that individual can never be afflicted with evil of any kind. For he is with God and God is with him. When, however, he abandons Him, may he be exalted, and is thus separated from God and God separated from him, he becomes in consequence of this a target for every evil that may happen to befall him. For the thing that necessarily brings about providence and deliverance from the sea of chance consists in that intellectual overflow.

When the bond with the overflow is disrupted, when the mind is no longer attending to the knowledge that guides and safeguards him and constitutes his advantage, the virtuous person is no better off in nature than the wicked person. They are both on their own, abandoned to the world, at the mercy of the elements, come what may.

> Yet an impediment may prevent from some time [the overflow] reaching the excellent and good man in question, or again it was not obtained at all by such and such imperfect and wicked man, and therefore the chance occurrences that befell them happened.

Full responsibility for the disconnection from the divine overflow lies with the individual, not God: "It is clear that we are the cause of this

---

[24] Maimonides thus rejects the suggestion that a truly virtuous person might experience undeserved suffering as part of a "trial"; see *Guide* III.24.

'hiding of the face', and we are the agents who produce this separation" (*Guide* III.51; Maimonides 1963: II.625–6).

Similarly, the prosperity of the wicked person is not a true flourishing, since this person is not enjoying the highest good, intellectual perfection, but only material fortune. Moreover, whatever prosperity may have come his way is totally undeserved and does not represent a reward (from God) for anything he has done. Rather, just as he is unprotected against the forces of nature, so it happens that chance has brought some apparently fine things his way. But his possession and enjoyment of them is equally subject to fortune and thus outside his control. It is also likely to be accompanied by unpleasant states of mind (anxiety, envy, fear) and certain to be short-lived.

Moral Luck

I want to conclude this chapter by stepping away from talk of divine providence – which may sound odd, even off-putting to nonreligious readers – and show how all of this is related to a millennia-old topic of philosophy, one that still receives a good deal of attention. There is another way to look at Maimonides' approach to the problem of evil, and it does not require any beliefs about God or theological views on the nature of evil.

The problem of moral luck concerns the extent to which one's flourishing is subject to factors beyond one's control.[25] In this context, "flourishing" refers to more than just a person's own subjective satisfaction with the way his life is going and his sense of success and fulfillment – which, on one common view, is what happiness amounts to. It refers also to a more objective condition of human well-being, where one's physical, intellectual, and emotional faculties are working at a kind of peak health and efficiency and can be assessed as such from an external perspective. "Flourishing" also refers to the moral judgments that others make as to whether one has, in acting and living, done well or ill. The question of moral luck, in this respect, concerns whether one should be held morally responsible (praiseworthy or blameworthy) for

---

[25] On moral luck, see Williams 1976 (where he coined the term) and Nagel 1979.

things that were unintentional, even involuntary, or for actions the outcome of which could not in any way have been foreseen or avoided.

As for the factors that may be beyond one's control, these will certainly involve momentary accidents; for example, did you intend to knock the other person down, or did you just happen to trip on the sidewalk and fall into them? But they should also include more consequential circumstances, such as where and to whom you are born, what opportunities for education and income were available to you, and so on. What bearing do all of these have on the assessment of how a person has fared?

The role of luck in our moral lives was a topic of great interest in antiquity. The Greek dramatists – Aeschylus, Sophocles, Euripides – created works in which luck plays a significant role in the characters' pursuit of happiness. In their "tragic" view of life, very often one's wellbeing can be significantly set back by unforeseen, haphazard factors. As one scholar puts it, goodness was seen by these poets as something "fragile" and subject to being overthrown by circumstance.[26] The classic case referenced in many philosophical analyses of moral luck is Oedipus. Had he not happened to be on that particular road at that particular time, his confrontation with another traveler would not have led to his loss of temper and, ultimately, his killing of that traveler. Still, we hold Oedipus morally responsible for the murder just because it resulted from his own irascible character. What made things worse, however, was that, unbeknownst to Oedipus, the unfortunate traveler/victim happened to be his father. So it was not just murder, it was the more serious crime of patricide. The consequences of this fortuitous encounter will, in the end, lead to Oedipus' downfall. The King of Thebes is a victim of moral (bad) luck.

The ancient philosophers took a different view. They believed that with the right intellectual and emotional training, one might achieve greater control over the course of one's life. The role of luck in securing happiness or flourishing (what they called *eudaimonia*) could thereby be mitigated, and even (as some believed) eliminated altogether. The key, according to Plato, Aristotle, and Stoics such as Epictetus, was the cultivation of virtue (although they disagreed among themselves on

---

[26] Nussbaum 1986.

what exactly virtue was, how it was acquired, and how the different virtues related to each other). Later, modern philosophers, too, have argued that a person should be held morally responsible, and thus subject to normative evaluation, only for what is under her control. Thus, Kant insists that whether a person is good or bad, and therefore deserving of moral praise or blame, is to be determined solely by the character of her will, not in any successes or failures she may experience in putting that will into practice (which may be subject to circumstances outside her control). He proclaims that "there is nothing that could possibly be conceived in the world ... that can be called good, without qualification, than a good will."[27] A person with a good will – who is motivated and intends to do her moral duty just because it is her moral duty – but who is a bit of a practical klutz and therefore incompetent in carrying out what she wants is still a good person, on Kant's reckoning.

Maimonides is definitely in the philosophers' camp on this question. In his view, the virtuous person who not only develops the right moral character but achieves the epistemic condition of intellectual perfection can reduce the extent to which chance affects her well-being and her doing well. Maimonides says this person is covered by divine providence. But what this really amounts to – and perhaps his talk of "providence" should be taken as metaphorical – is the reduction, if not elimination, of luck in her flourishing. As we have seen, the virtuous person's mind is fixated on the true and lasting good, and she thereby becomes immune to the lure of mutable goods and inured to the travails of her body. She also has the knowledge and skills by which she can navigate any dangers that nature may bring her way or any threats to her health and happiness that might arise by human design. She has achieved a lasting state of spiritual well-being and happiness that is not subject to fortune. The intellectually or rationally virtuous person is "protected." No longer "abandoned to chance," as Maimonides puts it, she is less subject to the evils – the pains, sadness, and disappointments – that, typically, fortuitously come our way. "Neither those that are consequent upon the nature of our being nor those that are due to the plotting of man will occur" (*Guide* III.51; Maimonides 1963: II.626). And whatever harms do ultimately touch her disturb her hardly at all.

---

[27] These are the opening lines of Chapter One of his *Groundwork of the Metaphysics of Morals*.

Why Be Good?

At the beginning of this chapter, I made the claim that without God there is no problem of evil. This is true if the problem is understood in its traditional sense, as a conundrum about reconciling the existence of an omnipotent, omniscient, and benevolent God with the presence of evils and imperfections in that deity's creation. But we can look at the problem in a way that requires no theological premises.

A central question of moral philosophy concerns motivation: Why should I be good? And *that* question is often understood in terms of egoistic consequences: What advantages will virtue bring *me*? Even without a providential God, and even recognizing that nature is indifferent to us – as those who have had storms ruin their picnic plans know – it is not unreasonable for a person to expect that being good is somehow in their own interest. Surely, we tend to think, being a good person carries some reward – not necessarily a material reward, of course, but at the very least a greater degree of happiness or well-being, or even just fewer bad things. Maimonides' response to this is: yes, that is correct. Virtue does have its rewards, not because there is a God who will dispense those rewards upon you, either in the here-and-now or some world-to-come, but because being virtuous has its benefits – in *this* life. It is good to be a good person. It is a better life.

CHAPTER 4

Judaism within the Limits of Reason

In Plato's early dialogue *Euthyphro*, we find Socrates on the eve of the trial in 399 BCE that will end with his conviction and, eventually, execution. According to the story, the official charges brought against him by some leading citizens of Athens are "failing to recognize the city's gods, introducing other new divinities, and breaking the law because he corrupts the youth of the city." However, Socrates knows – and we know – that the real reason for his indictment is political. Besides cavorting with individuals suspected of being enemies of the democracy, he has earned the resentment and suspicion of powerful citizens after years of harassing Athenians about the lives they were leading. Socrates has a bad reputation, in part because of those he refers to as the "old accusers" – people such as Aristophanes, whose unflattering portrayal of Socrates among the youth in plays like *The Clouds* (produced in 423 BCE) only reinforced the animus against him.

As the dialogue opens, Socrates is preparing to face his accusers and answer the charges. On his way to court for a preliminary hearing, he encounters his friend Euthyphro, who is also occupied with a serious legal matter. When Euthyphro's father discovered that one of his laborers had killed another man, he bound the killer "hand and foot" and threw him into a ditch while awaiting word from a priest on what to do. The laborer eventually died from exposure, and Euthyphro is now prosecuting his father for murder. Socrates is taken aback by this news and asks the young man how he could do something so audacious and apparently unfilial as to charge his own father with a serious crime. Euthyphro, who claims to have "accurate knowledge of all such things," replies that "what I am doing is the pious thing to do, prosecuting a wrongdoer . . . whether the wrongdoer is your father or your mother or anyone else; not prosecuting is impious."[1]

To determine whether Euthyphro is, in fact, justified in believing that prosecuting his father is a pious action, Socrates challenges him to state exactly what piety is; for if he does not know what piety itself is, then he cannot be certain that what he is doing is pious. The cocksure Euthyphro, convinced that he can satisfy Socrates' request, confidently responds that the pious is defined simply as what the gods love. "What is pleasing to the gods is pious, and what is not pleasing to them is impious."

Socrates cannot accept the claim that something is pious just because the gods love it. After all, if the gods disagree in their love of something, such that some gods love it and other gods hate it – and we know from Homer's tales that the Greek gods most certainly do fight over such matters – then one and the same thing would be both pious and impious, which is absurd. Socrates suggests that, on the contrary, the gods, because they are generally rational beings, will love a thing only because they find something to appreciate in it, some property of it that makes it worthy of their affection. The gods do not capriciously direct their love toward one thing or another. Rather, they love something only because there is some reason why they should love it. They love it, that is, because it is inherently lovable. Thus, Socrates insists, piety, far from being determined by the gods' favor, should be defined by that property or set of properties that all pious things share, that makes them pious, and that therefore causes those things to be loved by the gods. As he finally gets Euthyphro himself to admit, it is not that something is pious because the gods love it, but the gods love something only because they see that it is pious.

The general philosophical issue at play in the dialogue's debate over whether something is pious because it is loved by the gods or the gods love something because it is in itself pious has come to be known as the Euthyphro Problem. Are our most important values and the judgments based on them objectively grounded in the natures of things? Or, on the other hand, are they subjectively based on the predilections of some authority? To put the problem in terms more familiar to the Abrahamic

---

[1] Plato, *Euthyphro* 9d.

religious tradition: Does God make or do something because it is good, or is something good just because God does it? The Hebrew Bible says that on each day of creation God surveyed what he had done and "saw that it was good." But did God choose to create what he did because he perceived it to be inherently good? Or was what God created good simply because God created it – with the implication that had God created something entirely different, then *that* would have been good instead?

Central questions of philosophy, theology, morality, and politics depend on how one resolves the dilemma. If Euthyphro is right and something is good simply because God loves it, then goodness and many other values, while they may appear objective to us, are ultimately arbitrary and subjective. Whatever God loves is, by that fact alone, pious or good. There can be no measure of piety or goodness independent of God's will or favor that might objectively and rationally incline his love one way or another. This is because nothing is good or right (or true or just or pious or beautiful) in itself, but a thing becomes such only when God's preference so determines it. On the Socratic view, by contrast, because what is pious or good is so independently of what God – or any rational agent – loves or desires or thinks, there is a universal, objective standard of goodness in the natures of things that explains or establishes why certain things are good (even though, as the Socratic dialogue reveals with its inconclusive ending, it may be a very difficult philosophical task to specify what exactly that standard is). These good things are what reasonable beings, including God, favor.

In the history of philosophy, few thinkers have followed Euthyphro down the path of absolute divine voluntarism. Even medieval philosophers, for the most part deeply pious theologians who were concerned above all to explain and defend God's glory and power, usually stop short of saying that God's will alone is the source of all values and standards, of all goodness, beauty, and truth. The typical philosopher in the high middle ages – such as Thomas Aquinas in the thirteenth century – stresses the objective wisdom and intelligence of God's ways, with the divine reason, informed by eternal and uncreated truths and values, having primacy over, and providing guidance and motivation for, the divine will.² What God does, he does because he sees that it is good to do; it is not good just because He chooses to do it.

Obeying the Law

The Euthyphro Problem has great crossover appeal. There are many contexts in which it can be asked whether some value or rule or directive has its normative or obligatory force – its "oughtness" – for no other reason than that an authority has proclaimed it. When we read Maimonides, and without assuming he was familiar in any way with Plato, we can see that he was concerned with the dilemma's implications for Jewish Law.³ On a Euthyphro-type "divine command" theory, the six hundred and thirteen commandments of the Torah get their normativity solely from the fact that they issue from God. Just as something would be morally right ("pious," as Euthyphro would say) and thus morally obligatory because God "loves" or commands it – and the assumption is that we owe obedience to God – so all the *mitzvot* of the Torah, whether moral, liturgical, agricultural, dietary, and so on, constitute the *law* and ought to be followed only because they come from God. End of story.

For certain rationalist philosophers in the Jewish tradition, however, this is not the end of the story. In their view, it is perfectly legitimate to ask: Why does God command these laws rather than others? They assume that because God's activity is a kind of rational agency, there must be reasons for the laws, and they want to know what those reasons are. The ultimate source of the laws, then, would lie not in the absolute, arbitrary will of God but in the reasons for which God issued them. In that case, too, the ultimate normativity of the laws *for us* would derive not from the fact that they were chosen by God – although that remains a rather crucial part of the

---

² At the same time, Aquinas also insists on an identity of will and wisdom in God: "In God, power, essence, will, intellect, wisdom, and justice are one and the same" (*Summa Theologiae*, Ia, Q. 25, art. 5, rep. 1).
³ As should be clear in what follows, my concern in this chapter is with Maimonides' account of *divine law*, the Law handed down by God to Moses, not the laws (*nomoi*) created by human beings in political communities. On the distinction between the two, their origins and purposes, in Maimonides, see Galston 1978.

story – but because there is something reasonable about them. If we rational creatures should ask *why* we ought to obey the laws, even as we believe that they are set forth by God, it is because we are generally moved by reasons we can understand ("Do this for the sake of . . . ") rather than the brute fact of divine command ("God says do this, period!"). This is true even if the actual psychological motivation at work in some particular pious person for obeying the law is simply hope of God's reward or fear of God's judgment.

Of course, it all depends on what it means for laws to be "rational," or at least for us to see them as reasonable and thus to recognize their authority. It could be that the laws are "logically" rational in the sense that they are consistent, both individually (with no law being self-contradictory) and relationally, as a set (with no law contradicting another law). But this minimal sense of the rationality or reasonableness of the laws seems to be too weak to do the normative work necessary. Just because the laws are consistent and coherent, one could still ask: Why should I obey them?

There is another sense in which the laws might be logically rational: when they follow logically (deductively) from some higher principles that are broadly accepted. For example, a shared conception of justice might set constraints on what laws are permissible, and perhaps even imply particular laws (e.g., laws about the fair distribution of rights or property). In this case, what gives the laws their authority and their reasonableness are the higher principles themselves. And yet, this simply moves the question to another level: What is it about those principles that gives *them* their authority, such that their normativity – their "oughtness" – is inherited by the laws that follow from them?

At this point, we need more than logic to account for the laws and why they should be obeyed. To put it in a way amenable to Maimonides' account, we need to know why God chose these laws and not others, and the explanation must go beyond the fact that the laws are logically possible and logically consistent ones. Maimonides takes Socrates' side in his debate with Euthyphro. There is something special about the laws of Judaism, and that is why they are proclaimed by God.

Rationalism, Again

There has long been a kind of semi-rationalism at the heart of Jewish law. Traditionally, rabbinic Judaism has recognized among the commandments of the Torah a distinction between *mishpatim*, judgments or ordinances, and *huqqim*, ritual laws or edicts.[4] *Mishpatim* are divine commandments for which reasons independent of divine authority can be given. Among these are ranked the commandments not to kill, not to commit adultery, and not to steal. The obvious reasonableness of such rules, their undeniable appeal to us as moral, social, and political beings, is supposed to provide them with a kind of additional normativity beyond what they derive from God's will. *Huqqim*, on the other hand, are said to have either no reasons at all or no reasons we can know[5], and to derive their normativity from God's will alone; we are to obey them solely on the basis of divine authority. Examples of *huqqim* are the commandments not to eat certain foods, not to mix certain materials in garments, and the wide variety of laws regulating Jewish ceremonial practice. Although some *huqqim* may indeed serve a divine purpose – for example, to separate the Israelites from surrounding peoples – their reasonableness is beyond our ken, and so contributes nothing to their obligatoriness.

A more robust strain of rationalism takes the Talmudic doctrine of *ta'amei ha-mitzvot*, or providing reasons for the commandments, one step further and insists that *all* of the laws of Judaism are reasonable, at least in their generalities if not also in their specifics. And the reasonableness of any commandment is grounded in some accessible and familiar standard – personal well-being, social harmony, political welfare – that provides an intellectually satisfying justification for it. Even the most mundane and apparently trivial *huqqim*, on this view, have reasons we can understand.

Just as he laid the groundwork for a rationalist approach to the reading of the Bible, so once again Saadya ben Joseph, the *gaon* of the Babylonian academy, leads the philosophical way for Maimonides and others and sets the benchmark for Jewish legal rationalism.

---

[4] See, for example, the discussion in *Babylonian Talmud*, Yoma 67b.
[5] This is how Stern (1986) frames the distinction.

Saadya begins by distinguishing between two classes of Law. The first class comprises those laws that are in principle discoverable by reason alone, although we know them primarily because God has commanded them; the second class are those laws that are discoverable only by divine revelation. Included in the first class, which Saadya calls "the rational laws," are the most important moral commandments that govern our direct behavior toward God and toward other human beings. Reason or speculation confirms as necessary such principles as that a benefactor should be respected by having his kindness returned or by being thanked, that a wise person (and even more so the Creator) should not allow himself to be vilified and treated with contempt, that human beings should be forbidden from trespassing upon one another's rights by aggression, and that a wise person should be permitted to employ a worker and pay him wages.[6] A number of the Torah's commandments fall under one or another of these general ethical principles "dictated by reason." Thus, the commandment to know God and serve him with a sincere heart is an instantiation of the first principle; the commandment not to take God's name in vain is an example of the second; the prohibitions against stealing and dealing falsely with others represent applications of the third; and so on. While these are, of course, things that God commands us to do or not to do through revelation, Saadya insists that God has also "implanted approval of them in our reason." In a somewhat Kantian vein, whereby the ethical permissibility of an action is determined by whether or not it could be universalized and all people commanded or allowed to act in that way, Saadya notes that

> Theft was forbidden by wisdom because, if it were permitted, some men would rely on stealing the others' wealth, and they would neither till the soil nor engage in any other lucrative occupation. And if all were to rely on this source of livelihood, even stealing would become impossible, because, with the disappearance of all property, there would be absolutely nothing in existence that might be stolen.[7]

---

[6] Saadya 1948:138–9.
[7] Saadya 1948:141–2. Kant argues in his ethical writings that a law that allows for false promises would defeat the practice of making false promises, since trust – a necessary condition for making a false promise, which needs to be believed to work – would disappear.

The laws of the second class ("the revelational laws") concern "things neither the approval nor the disapproval of which is decreed by reason, on account of their own character ... matters regarding which reason passes no judgment in the way either of approval or disapproval so far as their essence is concerned ... The second class of laws concerns such matters as are of a neutral character from the point of view of reason."[8] Strictly speaking, then, they are distinct from the rational laws. Among the "acts which from the standpoint of reason are optional" are those related to the consecration of days and seasons, the cleanliness and uncleanliness of foods and materials, and ritual purity. And yet, Saadya insists, even these commandments have a reason. "Our Lord has given us an abundance of such commandments and prohibitions in order to increase our reward and happiness through them." What Saadya means is that in issuing the apparently nonrational revelational commandments for us to obey or disobey, God still had a purpose, namely, to make it possible for us to *earn* divine favor.

But Saadya goes further. While the revelational laws, especially in their specific details, may not have any clear and immediate rational justification by way of the principles outlined above – why, for example, are the Jewish people supposed to refrain from certain foods but not others? – nonetheless, they, too, like the rational laws, have a kind of utility.

> Thus the second [class of laws] might be attached secondarily to the first division [of the laws of the Torah]. One cannot help noting, upon deeper reflection, that they have some partial uses as well as a certain slight justification from the point of view of reason, just as those belonging to the first division have important uses and great justification from the point of view of reason.[9]

Speaking of the ceremonial and other nonmoral laws – distinguishing the Sabbath from the other days of the week, the selection of certain individuals to be leaders and prophets, the avoidance of sexual intercourse with certain people or at certain times – Saadya insists that while "the chief reason for the fulfillment of these principal precepts and their derivatives and whatever is connected with them is the fact that they

---

[8] Saadya 1948: 140. [9] Saadya 1948: 141.

represent the command of our Lord and enable us to reap a special advantage, yet I find that most of them have as their basis partially useful purposes."[10] Thus, the sanctification of the Sabbath day and the prohibition against work on it affords us the important opportunity to rest and relax and take time for study.

We can be certain, then, that *all* of the commandments are ultimately rational, in either a strong or a weak sense, even if their reasonableness is not always evident to us. All the "revealed precepts ... are, to a large extent at least, partially justified and possess much utilitarian value, although the wisdom and the view that the Creator had in mind in decreeing them is far above anything that men can grasp."[11] While the normative force of the second class of laws derives from God's authority rather than the approval of reason, they too are not without their utilitarian reasonableness. There is apparently no law that God commands arbitrarily and capriciously.

Now one might justifiably ask why, if Saadya is right, is revelation necessary? In the case of the second class of laws, revelation is absolutely necessary for their discovery. Reason may find some utility in them once they have been proclaimed, but reason alone could never have come up with these commandments and prohibitions. But, Saadya insists, revelation is essential also for the first class of laws, the rational laws. Even though reason by itself might discover the general principles they represent – such as the need to refrain from theft or adultery for the sake of peace and social harmony – revelation is needed to specify the particular manner in which the commandments are to be carried out. "[The rational precepts] are carried out practically only when there are messengers to instruct men concerning them."[12] Thus, while reason commands us to respect God and show gratitude toward him, it does not, by itself, tell us in what manner and at what times we are to do so. And while reason disapproves of adultery, it does not provide any guidance as to how a man and a woman become legally united as husband and wife and what this implies about their relations.

Moreover, revelation serves an important purpose even with respect to the general features of the rational commandments. Left to our own devices, through reason alone, we probably would have discovered these

---

[10] Saadya 1948: 143. [11] Saadya 1948: 145. [12] Saadya 1948: 145.

rules by ourselves, especially once society has been established. But it might have taken us a very, very long time to do so; in some cases, in fact – either because of distraction, incapacity, laziness, or other impediments – the laws might never have been discovered at all. And such moral commandments and prohibitions are much too important for individual and social well-being to have their implementation delayed or left to chance.

> Inasmuch as all matters of religious belief, as imparted to us by our Master, can be attained by means of research and correct speculation, what was the reason that prompted [divine] wisdom to transmit them to us by way of prophecy and support them by means of visible proofs and miracles rather than intellectual demonstrations? ... We say, then, that the All-Wise knew that the conclusions reached by means of the art of speculation could be attained only in the course of a certain measure of time. If, therefore, He had referred us for our acquaintance with His religion to that art alone, we would have remained without religious guidance whatever for a while, until the process of reasoning was completed by us so that we could make use of its conclusions.

This is where revelation has come to our assistance. "Even if it should take a long time for one of us who indulges in speculation to complete his speculation, he is without worry."[13]

Law's Wisdom

Maimonides is not satisfied with pointing out merely the general purposes of the Law. He goes beyond Saadya and devotes twenty-five chapters of the *Guide* to a closely argued and detailed examination of the rationality and utility of all of the commandments of the Torah, from the most important and consequential to those that might seem to deal with rather trivial matters. Just as his monumental *Mishneh Torah* offers a categorization and distilled summary of the rabbinic code, simplified and without all the disputes, explanations, and nonlegal material (*aggadah*) found in the Talmud, so these sections of the *Guide* present an equally systematic series of rational justifications of the various categories of law.

---

[13] Saadya 1948: 31–32.

Maimonides breaks down the commandments of Torah into thirteen classes, and insists that every single one of them "has a cause," "a reason," or "utility" and "conforms to wisdom." All of the laws of Judaism serve some useful purpose or other that human reason – in principle, if not always in fact – can fathom. This is because the Law has been instituted by God, who, for Maimonides, is directed by goodness and wisdom in all that he does and who is incapable of doing anything that is "vain, futile or frivolous." A vain action, Maimonides explains, is an action by which "its agent aims at some end and that end is not achieved, its achievement being hindered by obstacles." A futile action is an action which aims at no end whatsoever – Maimonides gives the example of playing with one's hands while thinking – while a frivolous action aims at a low or base end, such as carnal pleasure. None of these kinds of action may be attributed to God. "All his actions are good and excellent"; that is, they all have an end, the end is always a good and noble one, and they all succeed in realizing that end (*Guide* III.25; Maimonides 1963: II.502–3). This is true even when the purpose of some commandment is beyond our apprehension.

> All the Laws have a cause, though we do not know the causes for some of them and we do not know the manner in which they conform to wisdom. ... There is a cause for all the commandments; I mean to say that any particular commandment or prohibition has a useful end. In the case of some of them, it is clear to us in what way they are useful. ... In the case of others, their utility is not clear.

He gives examples of both clearly purposive laws and laws whose purpose is opaque to us.

> Any particular commandment or prohibition has a useful end. In the case of some of them, it is clear to us in what way they are useful – as in the case of the prohibition of killing and stealing. In the case of others, their utility is not clear – as in the case of the interdiction of the first products [of trees] and of [sowing] the vineyard with diverse seeds. Those commandments whose utility is clear to the multitude are called *mishpatim* [judgments], and those whose utility is not clear to the multitude are called *huqqim* [statutes]. (*Guide* III.26; Maimonides 1963: II.507)

Notice that what distinguishes the *huqqim* from the *mishpatim* is not, as some rabbinic authorities claim, the lack of reasons for the former but rather the accessibility of such reasons to the multitude.

Like Saadya, Maimonides says that the reasonableness of any law is most readily seen in its generality. And yet, he insists, even the particularities of the laws often have a clear utility. Take, for example, commandments that direct precisely how an animal must be slaughtered. Should one ask generally why animals are to be killed, it is obviously so that we may eat and survive. But if the question is why they should be killed in one way rather than another – such as cutting the throat in a certain manner – the answer, though not obvious, would be that this insures a quicker and more humane death, "the easiest death in the easiest manner." He concedes, however, that in the case of the very particular details of some laws, a cause or a reason cannot ultimately be found. But even this lack of a cause is not without its own reason: "No cause will ever be found for the fact that one particular sacrifice consists in a lamb and another in a ram ... Know that wisdom rendered it necessary that there should be particulars for which no cause can be found" (*Guide* III.26; Maimonides 1963: II.509). *Some* animal had to be sacrificed, and so a choice had to be made, but the choice by God of a lamb rather than a ram was ultimately and explicably an arbitrary one.

According to Maimonides, the Law serves two main purposes. First, it contributes to the well-being of the body, broadly understood to include both physical health and general safety. Through its plethora of moral, communal, dietary, and ceremonial regulations – "Do not steal," "Do not kill," "Do not commit adultery," along with prohibitions against eating certain animals or mixing particular foods, and so on – the commandments seek to foster good physical condition, abolish "reciprocal wrongdoing," and establish a stable and supportive domestic, social, and political environment. All of these are necessary conditions for individual flourishing.

> Man has two perfections: a first perfection, which is the perfection of the body, and an ultimate perfection, which is the perfection of the soul. The first perfection consists in being healthy and in the very best bodily state, and this is only possible through his finding the things necessary for him whenever he seeks them. These are his food and all the other things needed for the governance of his body, such as a shelter, bathing, and so forth. (*Guide* III.27; Maimonides 1963: II.511)

Moreover, the expressly ethical commandments are meant to do more than just keep a person from doing this or that bad thing on this or that occasion. Following these laws through habitual practice leads an individual to develop the moral virtues and acquire the excellence of character that, as we have seen, is an essential step on the way to the ultimate perfection. Without a healthy body, secure living conditions, and good habits, the pursuit of wisdom is seriously hindered.

Second, the Law contributes directly to that ultimate perfection by fostering the welfare of the soul. It accomplishes this by communicating true beliefs, either directly (by proclaiming in propositional form that "God is one," "God rewards the good and punishes the wicked," "God is the creator and ought to be worshiped and loved and feared," and so on) or – and here "the Law" needs to be understood broadly to refer to all the elements of the Torah, including its narrative parts – through parables. The individual who, through a study of the "speculative opinions" embodied in the Law, acquires an understanding of natural science and metaphysical truths – which, as we have seen, is what "the knowledge of the Creator and His actions" amounts to – has become truly rational *in actu*. He has developed his intellect to the highest degree and has thereby perfected himself. This improvement of the soul is the supreme aim of the Law, and its ultimate rationale.

> Every commandment from among these six hundred and thirteen commandments exists either with a view to communicating a "correct opinion," to putting an end to an unhealthy opinion, to communicating a rule of justice, to warding off an injustice, to endowing men with a noble moral quality, or to warning them against an evil moral quality. Thus all [the commandments] are bound up with three things: opinions, moral qualities, and political civic actions ... Therefore we have limited ourselves here in giving reasons for every law to these three classes. (*Guide* III.31; Maimonides 1963: II.524)

Each commandment, then, deals with either the acquisition of knowledge, the development of individual good character, or the preservation of communal life. As Maimonides puts it, "all the commandments are bound up with three things: opinions, moral qualities, and political civic actions" (*Guide* III.31; Maimonides 1963: II.524). Through these means, our material welfare and our spiritual well-being are ensured.

Law's Wisdom

A few examples of what Maimonides has in mind will be helpful. The most obviously useful and purposive laws are those that concern our behavior with regard to each other. Imperatives against killing, stealing, false oaths, adultery, and such matters are, on any reasonable ethical theory, justified; an ethics that allowed for these sorts of action would hardly qualify as an ethics. But Maimonides also includes among the evidently reasonable commandments those that deal with self-regarding activities, those in which the only beneficial or deleterious effects are in the agent himself. Thus, laws concerning eating, drinking, and sex are all about "the abandonment, depreciation, and restraint of desires in so far as possible, so that these should be satisfied only in so far as this is necessary." Maimonides is not proposing any kind of asceticism. But he does believe that an important set of the Torah's laws are meant to steer us toward that middle course, the virtuous mean between extremes. The laws that direct our sustenance and most basic enjoyments are meant to turn us away from the unbridled pursuit of base pleasures, or what he calls "polluting moral qualities."

> You know already that most of the lusts and licentiousness of the multitude consist in an appetite for eating, drinking and sexual intercourse. This is what destroys man's last perfection [the perfection of the soul and intellect], but also harms him in his first perfection [perfection of body and character], and what corrupts most of the circumstances of the citizens and of the people engaged in domestic governance. For when only the desires are followed, as is done by the ignorant, the longing for speculation is abolished, the body is corrupted, and the man to whom this happens perishes before this is required by his natural term of life. (*Guide* III.33; Maimonides 1963: II.532)

Maimonides' view on this is not limited to the *Guide* but extends to the halakhic works as well. He notes in the "Eight Chapters" of the *Commentary on the Mishnah* that

> The Law did not lay down its prohibitions or enjoin its commandments except for just this purpose, namely, that by its disciplinary effects we may persistently maintain the proper distance from either extreme. For the restrictions regarding all the forbidden foods, the prohibition of illicit intercourse, the forewarning against prostitution, the duty of performing the legal marriage rites ... all of these God commanded in order that we should keep entirely distant from the extreme of the inordinate

indulgence of the passions, and, even departing from the exact medium, should incline somewhat toward self-denial, so that there may be firmly rooted in our souls the disposition for moderation.

He adds that

if you should test most of the commandments from this point of view [i.e., the perspective of instilling moral qualities], you would find that they are all for the discipline and guidance of the faculties of the soul. ("Eight Chapters," IV; Maimonides 1972: 372–3)

In addition to those commandments that are meant to improve us morally by directly regulating behavior through prescribing or prohibiting certain kinds of actions and thus fostering the virtues of character – thereby also laying the groundwork for the intellectual virtues – there are those commandments that do the moral job by communicating fundamental true beliefs. These include beliefs about God – for example, that God stands in providential judgement over us – and beliefs about ethical matters. Thus, one should know the importance of repentance, since anyone who believed that repentance is futile and that their sinful behavior was beyond remedy would have no motive to turn from his evil ways. "He would persist in his error and sometimes perhaps disobey even more because of the fact that no stratagem remains at his disposal. If, however, he believes in repentance, he can correct himself and return to a better and more perfect state than the one he was in before he sinned" (*Guide* III.36; Maimonides 1963: II.540). Similarly, the commandments about lending and borrowing, the sabbatical year, and the selling of land are meant to encourage the belief that we should pity "the weak and the wretched" and be charitable to the poor, and even see that it is in our own best interest to do so. Laws concerning property, Maimonides notes, teach us principles about justice and fairness. "[They] regard the transactions that of necessity occur between people and see to it that these do not deviate from a course of mutual help useful for both parties, lest one of them should aim at increasing his share in the whole and at being the gainer in all respects" (*Guide* III.42; Maimonides 1963: II.568).

Modern readers may be surprised to find that Maimonides' utilitarian account of the laws of Judaism extends even to the most peculiar dietary restrictions. The prohibitions against the consumption of pork products and the mixing of meat and dairy also have their purposes in both bodily health and spiritual well-being.

> Among all those [foods] forbidden to us, only pork and fat may be imagined not to be harmful. But this is not so, for pork is more humid than is proper and contains much superfluous matter. The major reason why the Law abhors it is its being very dirty and feeding on dirty things ... If swine were used for food, market places and even houses would have been dirtier than latrines ... You know the dictum of the Sages, may their memory be blessed: "The mouth of the swine is like walking excrement."

The rabbi/physician adds that "the fat of the intestines makes us full, spoils the digestion, and produces cold thick blood." As for the prohibition against eating "meat boiled in milk" – that is, consuming animal flesh and milk products in proximity – Maimonides surmises that this had something to do with idolatry insofar as the surrounding tribes, from whom the Israelites needed to distinguish themselves, probably performed ceremonies that involved that practice. Regarding ritual butchery according to the rules of *kashrut*, he notes that

> The commandment concerning the slaughtering of animals is necessary ... Since the necessity to have good food requires that animals be killed, the aim was to kill them in the easiest manner, and it was forbidden to torment them through killing them in a reprehensible manner by piercing the lower part of their throat or by cutting off one of their members ... It is likewise forbidden to slaughter it and its young on the same day, this being a precautionary measure in order to avoid slaughtering the young animal in front of its mother. For in these cases animals feel very great pain. (*Guide* III.48; Maimonides 1963: II.598–9)

Cruelty to animals is one step away from cruelty to human beings, and so these commandments are part of the Law's teaching of moral principles and inculcation of good character.

The Law, for Maimonides no less than for Saadya, is not an *a*rational body of *mitzvot* that find their only validation in the inscrutable decrees of God. While we still need to find a way to make sense of referring to what God "does" or "wills" or "orders" that is consistent with Maimonides' anti-anthropomorphic theology, we can say that his God does nothing by a brute, unmotivated act of will. There are no arbitrary – or futile – commandments that are not justified by their utility for a good life. Like Socrates' gods, Maimonides' deity is moved by wisdom and reason.

> [God] wills only what is possible, and not everything that is possible but only that which is required by His wisdom to be such ... None of our scholars and none of our men of knowledge believe that [the world] came about through the will and nothing else. (*Guide* III.25; Maimonides 1963: II.505)

There is no commandment, Maimonides insists, that cannot find its "approval" and even its demonstration in reason. According to tradition, the Law is first received through revelation and handed down by the prophets. But this does not abrogate the obligation to seek the "verification" of the Law in a rational science and "correct speculation" on its foundations. "Man is first required to obtain knowledge of the Torah, then to obtain wisdom ... The opinions in question should first be known as being received through tradition; then they should be demonstrated" (*Guide* III.54; Maimonides 1963: II.633–4).

God's aim in everything he does, whether in creation or in legislating, comes down to bringing into existence as much of what is good as possible. Unlike Euthyphro's gods, the Maimonidean God loves and chooses something *because* it is good.

God as Lawgiver?

In light of the earlier discussion of Maimonides' conception of God, which discouraged thinking of God in anthropomorphic terms, one might wonder how to understand all this talk of a rational God moved by wisdom to issue commandments and lay down laws. Read literally, it seems inconsistent with what Maimonides has to say about the nature of God. A God who does something in light of principled reflection and choice would appear to operate very much as we do. But Maimonides is insistent that there can be no comparison whatsoever between God and human beings, neither in nature nor in agency. How, then, can we reconcile these things?

In the previous chapter, I suggest that Maimonides' talk of divine providence might be read figuratively or metaphorically. His God is not a kind of person or agent who deliberates, makes decisions, or executes judgment by actively issuing rewards and punishments. As I read Maimonides, his God does not literally *do* anything. Rather, what providence really amounts to, in the *Guide* at least, is the natural consequences of knowledge. The person devoted to perfecting his moral character and then his intellect will enjoy a kind of protection from the vicissitudes of nature, from moral luck. He will be better prepared than others to navigate his way safely through the world and successfully through life. He will flourish.

Perhaps something similar can be done with Maimonides' discussion of the Law. Thus, the more sophisticated reader of the *Guide* should accept that the author of the commandments of the Torah was not literally some personal God but an inspired prophet – Moses – writing "in the language of man." Obedience to the laws by the multitude, essential for political and religious community, would be more likely if they believed that the laws were proclaimed by a providential deity to be feared. We know from Maimonides' discussion of prophecy that what distinguished the ancient prophets from the ordinary run of human beings was their combination of philosophical knowledge, superb moral character, and perfected imaginations. Who better, then, to craft laws calculated to promote ethical behavior, communicate truths, unite unruly tribes into a nation, and establish a secure and stable society – and to do so through inspiring and edifying narratives? What appears in their stories as "commandments" and "laws" issued by an anthropomorphic, providential God is just their imaginative formulation of the knowledge that they, as recipients of the "divine overflow," understand through their intellects.

On Disobedience

As Maimonides knows – as anyone knows, and as the Bible's narratives show time and again – disobedience of the Law is all too easy and all too frequent. But in Maimonides' view, not all disobedience is the same. He makes an interesting distinction between different kinds of transgression, a distinction that is grounded in either the voluntariness of the transgression or the motivations of the transgressor.

> Know that with regard to the perpetration of things forbidden by the Law there are four categories: the first being that of the compelled transgressor; the second that of the inadvertent transgressor; the third that of the deliberate transgressor; the fourth that of him who transgresses in a high-handed manner. (*Guide* III.41; Maimonides 1963: II.563)

The first two kinds of transgression are involuntary or unintentional. The compelled transgressor does not generally want to violate the Law, nor does he intend to do so on this occasion. If his transgression is forced by circumstances beyond his control – a threat to his life or some act of nature – then, Maimonides concludes, "he should not be punished and no sin whatever lies upon him." The inadvertent transgressor is someone whose act is voluntary but unintentionally a sin because he either does not know of the prohibition or, knowing the prohibition, is unaware that what he is doing is an instance of the kind of act that is prohibited. He is somewhat more responsible for his transgression, "for if he had made efforts to be firm and cautious there would have been no inadvertence on his part." His ignorance is culpable. He should have endeavored to know the Law or paid more attention to what he was doing – for example, he should have known that the meal he was eating contained both meat and dairy. While this individual should not be subject to punishment, he does have to atone for his action.

The third and fourth kinds of transgression, by contrast, are informed and intentional – the transgressors know full well what they are doing – but distinguished one from the other by the motive behind the transgression. The deliberate transgressor knows the Law and is aware that he is in violation of it, but is so moved by his excessive desire for something (wealth, pleasure, honor) that he is willing to risk the consequences of his sin. Such an individual, suffering from a kind of weakness of will – he knows that what he is doing is wrong, but he cannot help himself – is subject to both blame and punishment. (It is unclear whether Maimonides would put in this class the case of someone who is destitute and starving and has no alternative but to steal some food for himself and his children.)

Worst of all, however, is the high-handed transgressor. This is the individual who violates the commandments not in order to obtain some further end but just because they are the commandments. He is ornery, despises the law, and the object of his desire is the transgression for its own sake. "Such a one does not transgress merely because of desire or because, on account of his evil character, he wishes to obtain things that are forbidden by the Law, but in order to oppose and combat the Law" (*Guide* III.41; Maimonides 1963: II.565). The goal of the high-handed transgressor is nothing less than "to ruin and oppose the Law itself." For this reason, the only appropriate punishment, Maimonides says, is death.

If there is a hierarchy of guilt, there is also, inversely, a hierarchy of praiseworthiness. Consider two kinds of moral agent, each of whom always does the right thing. One acts well because that just is her nature. Her character is such that, habituated to the mean, she always knows what it is best to do, has a strong desire or inclination to do it, and even takes pleasure in so acting. She is like Aristotle's virtuous person. Another agent also always does what is right, but takes no pleasure in doing so. In fact, he must struggle against his inclinations, which are selfish and pleasure-seeking. His nature moves him toward what ethics forbids, and yet he forces himself to do what ethics requires.

Now, which of these two agents is, from a moral perspective, more praiseworthy? Which is more deserving of our admiration? Some might be tempted to argue that it is the latter. His ability to resist his baser urges is a sign of his strength of character. Despite not getting any pleasure from doing what is right, he does it anyway. Others will insist that it is the former, who is ethically admirable in a more well-rounded way – with her natural inclinations and feelings in alignment with her sense of judgment – and thus is a model moral agent.

In the "Eight Chapters," Maimonides steers a middle course between these two models. There is, first,

> the man of self-restraint [who] performs moral and praiseworthy deeds, yet he does them desiring and craving all the while for immoral deeds, but, subduing his passions and actively fighting against a longing to do those things to which his faculties, his desires, and his psychic disposition excite him, succeeds, though with a constant vexation and irritation, in acting morally.

By contrast, there is "the saintly man," who is "guided in his actions by that to which his inclination and disposition prompt him, in consequence of which he acts morally from innate longing and desire" ("Eight Chapters," VI; Maimonides 1972: 376). Maimonides notes that "the philosophers" – and he presumably means Aristotle and his followers – agree that the saintly person is superior, and that the inclinations of the person with self-restraint indicate "the presence of an immoral psychic disposition" and so he must be ranked "lower in the scale of virtue." On the other hand, "the rabbis" favor the person who must fight off his vicious urges.

> They consider him who desires iniquity and craves for it (but does not do it) more praiseworthy and perfect than the one who feels no torment at refraining from evil; and they even go so far as to maintain that the more praiseworthy and perfect a man is, the greater is his desire to commit iniquity and the more irritation does he feel at having to desist from it. ("Eight Chapters," V; Maimonides 1972: 377)

While the philosophers and the rabbis seem to be at irreconcilable odds here, Maimonides suggests that, in a sense, "both are correct." The rabbis are right to the extent that the urges that are forgivable but must be resisted are only inclinations to violate the ceremonial prohibitions, "such as partaking of meat and milk together, wearing clothes made of wool and linen, and entering in to consanguineous marriages." These sorts of actions are transgressions only because of the Law (although, as we have seen, the commandments regarding these have utilitarian justifications). If there were no Law, they would not be bad actions. Thus, there is nothing inherently wrong about having desires to do them. By contrast, there are the things that "all people agree are commonly evils" – such as murder, theft, causing injury to innocent people, ingratitude, disrespect of parents, and so on. Maimonides argues that these are bad actions in and of themselves, not merely because of the Law, and so should never be the object of desire.

> There is no doubt that a soul which has the desire for and lusts after these misdeeds is imperfect; that a noble soul has absolutely no desire for any such crimes and experiences no struggle in refraining from them. ("Eight Chapters," VI; Maimonides 1972: 378)

This account introduces yet another distinction among the commandments, namely, those that prescribe or prohibit actions that are absolutely criminal, and those that concern actions that are only relatively (to Jewish law) forbidden. A desire to perform the latter may be natural; a desire to perform the former, no matter how common, is the sign of a diseased soul.

Free Will and Responsibility

To hold any transgressor morally responsible for his transgression, as Maimonides does in three of the four cases, it is necessary that the agent acts freely in undertaking the forbidden action. Justice – human or divine – requires that punishment must be deserved, and only an agent who is free in doing what he does deserves to suffer consequences.

Of course, the challenge is to specify what it means for an agent to be free and for an act to be done freely. This question has long been the subject of philosophical dispute, with a particular focus on freedom of the will, that is, on the act of volition behind the action, the choosing to do something. Assuming that "hard determinism" is wrong and we allow that at least some of the things we do are "free," the debate has focused on whether freedom is compatible with any kind of determination. Can an act be free if it was determined to happen?

Proponents of libertarian freedom insist that freedom and determination are *in*compatible, and that for an act of will to be free it must not in any way have been irrevocably determined. What they mean by this is that, even if there were some factors inclining the agent in one direction over another, it must have been possible, all things being the same, for the agent to have chosen and acted otherwise. If one's belief that chocolate is the best flavor of ice cream and one's subsequent desire for chocolate ice cream move one to order chocolate ice cream at the shop, it still must have been possible, even with these mental factors in play, for one to have ordered vanilla.

The proponent of compatibilism (also called "soft determinism") agrees that there are some actions (some volitions) that are free, even if they are determined and could not have been otherwise. It all depends on what is doing the determining. A person who orders chocolate because there is a gun to his head is, just because of that external threat and constraint, not choosing freely. But if a person orders chocolate because there is something about *himself*, some internal factors – his personality, his beliefs and values, his present mental state – that causes him to do so, then even if, with all those personal factors in play, he could not have done otherwise, his choice was free. It was *he* who made the choice, not someone threatening him.

Maimonides seems to waiver between a libertarian conception of freedom and a compatibilist one.[14]

Much of the Maimonidean cosmos is absolutely determined. The rotational motions of the heavenly spheres and the directions overflowing from God down through the separate intellects play a causal role in the constitution of natural things and their law-like behaviors. This comes about especially by the ways in which the celestial factors "necessitate" the mixture of the primary forms of nature (heat, cold, dryness, and moisture) and, subsequently, of the elements (earth, air, fire, and water) in composite things. In fact, all of inanimate nature is governed by deterministic laws. Even the bodies of human beings, like all physical objects, are subject to the forces that derive from both the motions of the spheres and the natural tendencies of the elements.

But what about what takes place within the human mind? The deliberations we undertake, the decisions and choices we make, the volitions on which we act – are these, too, subject to the deterministic forces that govern most of the cosmos? Or do they escape that causal network and remain undetermined in such a way that they did not have to occur the way they did and could have been otherwise?

There is a strong libertarian strain in Maimonides' thinking on free will, especially in his halakhic writings. In the *Mishneh Torah*, *Hilkhot Teshuvah* (Laws of Repentance), he states boldly that "free will is granted to all men. If one desires to turn himself to the path of good and be righteous, the choice is his. Should he desire to turn to the path of evil and be wicked, the choice is his" (V.1). He adds, in the same chapter, that only a fool believes that "at the time of a man's creation, God decrees whether he will be righteous or wicked ... There is no one who compels him, sentences him or leads him towards either of these two paths. Rather, he, on his own initiative and decision, tends to the path he chooses" (V.2).

Similarly, in the "Eight Chapters," we read that

> man's conduct is entirely in his own hands. No compulsion is exerted upon man, and no external influence is brought to bear that would

---

[14] For Maimonides on human freedom, see Gellman 1989, Sokol 1998, and Pines 1960.

constrain him to be either virtuous or vicious ... Man has full sway over all his actions. If he wishes to do a thing, he does it; if he does not wish to do it, he need not, without any external compulsion controlling him.

We have, Maimonides insists, "freedom of choice." All of a person's actions "are subject to his free will and undoubtedly comply with or transgress God's commands; for ... the commands and prohibitions of the Law refer only to those actions which man has absolute free choice to perform or not to perform." When we choose to do or forbear from doing something, "there is no outside influence or restraint." "By and of himself man can distinguish between good and evil and do that which he pleases with absolutely no restraint ... It is an essential characteristic of man's makeup that he should of his own free will act morally or immorally, doing just as he chooses" ("Eight Chapters," VIII; Maimonides 1972: 379–84).

For Maimonides, divine omnipotence – God's infinite power and eternal decrees – does not interfere with human freedom of choice. There is no predestination in human affairs. Our actions, he says, are not governed by "the will and desire of God." But God's omnipotence is not the only potential threat to free will. There is also divine omniscience. An all-knowing God knows from eternity, with absolute certainty, all truths. These include truths about presumably contingent events that will occur in time, and especially what will happen to any of his creatures and what they will do. This applies as much to acts of human willing as to inanimate events in the physical world. But if God knows eternally and *infallibly* what a person will choose to do well before she chooses to do it, in what sense might she have chosen otherwise? Does not God's foreknowledge render her choice absolutely necessary, for all time? The difficulty is not that God's knowledge that a free choice will occur *causes* the event to happen but that God's knowledge means that the event cannot fail to happen (since God's beliefs cannot possibly be false). This is a classic problem in philosophical theology, often called the problem of future contingents (as it concerns preserving the contingency of events foreknown by God), addressed by numerous thinkers from the medieval period on. Here is how Maimonides frames the conundrum:

> Does God know or does he not know that a certain individual will be good or bad? If you say he knows, then it necessarily follows that man is

compelled to act as God knew beforehand he would act; otherwise, God's knowledge would be imperfect. If you say that God does not know in advance, then great absurdities and destructive religious theories will result. ("Eight Chapters," VIII; Maimonides 1972: 384)

Gersonides addresses the problem in an Aristotelian way, arguing that though God is omniscient, his knowledge simply does not extend to the choices of free agents. Maimonides rejects this approach. Rather, his response is, once again, simply to discourage thinking about God on the model of human agency and to emphasize the absolute inscrutability of God's ways. In human beings, to live is one thing and to know is another; knowledge is just an attribute we possess, and a changing one at that. But there can be no such distinction between being and attribute in God. All of God's attributes are one with God's being. So God knowing something cannot be compared to the way in which *we* know something.

> It is manifest that God is identical with his attributes, and his attributes with him, so that it may be said that he is the knowledge, the knower, and the known, and that he is the life, the living and the source of his own life, the same being true of his other attributes. ("Eight Chapters," VIII; Maimonides 1972: 385)

The upshot, once again, is that "we cannot comprehend God's knowledge." There is nothing meaningful we can say about the way in which God knows things. It is thus futile to try to reconcile, through reason, God's foreknowledge and human freedom. All we know is that there is such freedom, but any understanding of how God knows how we will exercise that freedom is beyond our reach.

Maimonides takes a similar skeptical/compatibilist approach in the *Guide*:

> [God's] knowledge, may he be exalted, that a certain possible thing will come into existence, does not in any way make that possible thing quit the nature of the possible. On the contrary, the nature of the possible remains with it; and knowledge concerning what possible things will be produced does not entail one of the two possibilities becoming necessary ... His knowledge concerning what will happen does not make this possible thing quit its nature [as possible]. However, this

constitutes a great difficulty for the apprehension of our inadequate intellects. (*Guide* III.20; Maimonides 1963: II.482)

In short, there is no philosophical resolution to this particular problem available to human reason.[15]

Still, notice that in all of the passages quoted above what Maimonides' conception of freedom rules out is "external compulsion" and "outside influence or restraint." What is especially excluded is God determining an individual to do this or that. But left unsaid is whether freedom is compatible with there being any *internal* factors that compel, determine, or restrain the will. Even if a person is free to do a thing *if he wishes to do it*, as the passage above indicates, the real question is whether the wish or willing to do it – the volition itself – is also free in the sense of undetermined.

That the answer to this question may be "no" is suggested by Maimonides' description of a person's character as made up of "moral dispositions," which incline him toward one kind of behavior or another. "One man is choleric, always irascible; another sedate, never angry ... One is a sensualist whose lusts are never sufficiently gratified; another is so pure in soul that he does not even long for the few things that our physical nature needs" (*Mishneh Torah, Hilkhot Deot* I.1; Maimonides 1972: 51). Virtues and vices are "psychic conditions and dispositions" which lead to conduct. If a person is of miserly character, he will act in miserly ways and be stingy with his charity. Is there a determinism at work here, one that operates from within the agent (as opposed to being a matter of external causes or constraint)? As Maimonides notes in the *Guide*, when discussing the different ways in which people transgress the Law, some do it "on account of [their] evil character" (*Guide* III.41; Maimonides 1963: II.565).

There are two possible ways of preserving a more libertarian reading of Maimonides. On the one hand, it may be that those "moral dispositions" of character incline without necessitating. Perhaps they make it very likely, even practically inevitable, that a person will act in such and such a way under certain circumstances, yet without completely foreclosing the possibility of the person choosing otherwise and acting

---

[15] For discussion of the problem of human freedom and divine foreknowledge, see Rudavsky 2010: 150–8 and Feldman 2008.

contrary to her character under the same circumstances. It is not impossible for a miserly person to resist their disposition and act generously (although they will not do so).

On the other hand, even if we allow that one's character makes it absolutely certain and unavoidable that one will act in a particular way – and so leave a kind of compatibilism in place with respect to particular volitions – it is clear from Maimonides' discussion of character and moral training that there is a sense in which our character is up to us and we are free (in a libertarian sense) to become this or that kind of person. While moral dispositions constitute "a fixed part of [a person's] character," whether or not a person has a virtuous character is something for which he is responsible. If you are of an immoral disposition, it is because you have freely chosen not to undertake the training and habituation that are necessary to become virtuous.

> It behooves man to accustom himself to the practice of good deeds until he acquires the virtues corresponding to those good deeds; and, furthermore, to abstain from evil deeds so that he may eradicate the vices that may have taken root in him. Let him not suppose that his characteristics have reached such a state that they are no longer subject to change, for any one of them may be altered from the good to the bad, and vice versa; and, moreover, all in accordance with his own free will. ("Eight Chapters," VIII; Maimonides 1972: 384)

If on any given occasion you sin, you sin freely, even though you are the kind of person naturally given to sin and so cannot *not* sin – just because you have chosen to be that kind of person, by not choosing to become a better person.[16]

Ultimately, Maimonides seems concerned to allow at least *some* room for true freedom of the will. Were our volitions compelled by causes, whether by external circumstances or by internal factors over which we have (or had) no control at all, we could not be held morally responsible for our actions. But if we are not morally responsible for what we do, then God could reasonably be accused of acting futilely and unjustly: futilely, because there would be no point in commanding us to do

---

[16] It is, of course, a further question as to whether a person once endowed with a sinful disposition *can* subsequently choose to become a better person, still has the capacity to start acting in virtuous ways so as to change that disposition.

certain things and not do other things if our doing them or not doing them was not up to us; and unjustly because, as God is supposed to reward us for our virtue and punish us for our sins, it would be wrong to hold us responsible for actions over which we have no control.

> Were a man compelled to act according to the dictates of predestination, then the commands and prohibitions of the Law would becomes null and void, and the Law would be completely false, since man would have no freedom in what he does . . . Reward and punishment would be pure injustice, both as regards man towards man and as between God and man. ("Eight Chapters," VIII; Maimonides 1972: 380)

The Validity of the Law

Spinoza, as we have seen, explicitly criticizes Maimonides' account of the interpretation of the Bible and his views on prophecy. He must also have Maimonides in mind – not to mention the entire rabbinic tradition – when he insists that Jewish law is no longer binding on latter-day Jews. Spinoza is said by some contemporaries, who claim to have spoken with him just a couple of years after his *herem*, to have confessed that he was expelled from the Amsterdam Portuguese-Jewish community because he was insisting that "the Law is false."[17] The witnesses do not tell us what exactly he meant by this claim. However, his discussion of Jewish law in the *Theological-Political Treatise*, begun less than ten years later, fills in some of the details.

Many of the commandments in the Hebrew Bible relate only to liturgical practices and regulations for a sectarian religious community. Spinoza insists that these were instituted by Moses under unique historical circumstances and for specific political aims: to motivate the ancient Israelites on their exodus from Egypt and to instill in them a sense of unity and purpose. These laws are thus of limited scope and validity. Unlike the true divine law – "Love your neighbor as yourself" – which is universally valid for all human beings, the ceremonial laws of Judaism are particularistic. The *mitzvot* of the Torah are directed only to a given people and adapted to their condition at a certain extended period in time.

[17] Nadler 2018: 160–2.

Ceremonies – at least those treated in the Old Testament – were instituted only for the Hebrews, and were so adapted to their state that for the most part they could be performed only by the whole society, not by each person. So it is certain that they do not pertain to the divine law, and make no contribution to blessedness and virtue, but concern only the election of the Hebrews – i.e., only the temporal happiness of the body and the peace of the state. For that reason, they could be useful only so long as their state lasted.[18]

The laws in question here include those concerning the priesthood, ritual purity, Temple sacrifice, and the worship of God, as well as the more routine legal, economic, social, and institutional directives that gave the Hebrew commonwealth its identity, strength, and stability. Especially important from a historical and political perspective are the regulations about property, diet, agriculture, clothing, and so on, which served to distinguish the Hebrew commonwealth and, later, the Israelite kingdom from surrounding nations.

Consequently, with the end of Israelite sovereignty and, especially, the final destruction of the Temple in Jerusalem in 70 CE, the laws instituted by Moses and the prophets have lost their raison d'être and, thus, their obligatory force. In exile, without a state of their own, the Jews have no obligation or even reason to obey Jewish law. The only laws to which they are justifiably subject are the laws of the state in which they live, as well as the law of nature – to love God and your fellow human beings and treat them with justice and charity – which prescribes the path to true blessedness.[19] "After the destruction of their state the Hebrews are not bound to perform ceremonies ... After their state was dissolved the Jews were no more bound by the law of Moses than they were before their social order and Republic began."[20] In

---

[18] *Theological-Political Treatise*, V; Spinoza 2016: 138.
[19] This raises the question of whether, with the re-establishment of a Jewish state in Israel, Jewish law has regained the political foundation that it lost with the end of the ancient kingdom. I suspect that Spinoza's answer to this is "no." First, without a rebuilding of the Temple and the reinstatement of Temple worship and a priestly caste, all of the commandments related to such matters remain obsolete. Second, the laws instituted by Moses and executed by later Israelite sovereigns were not just laws for *a* Jewish state but for the stability and prosperity of a particular Jewish state under specific historic and geopolitical conditions; these conditions no longer obtain, and so Mosaic law is no longer necessary to provide for the well-being of a Jewish state.
[20] *Theological-Political Treatise*, V; Spinoza 2016: 142.

Spinoza's view, Jewish law, for a seventeenth-century Jew (indeed, for all Jews after 70 CE), is anachronistic and obsolete.

If we may be permitted an anachronistic line of inquiry, Maimonides' response to Spinoza's claim that the laws of the Torah have lost their raison d'être would be a firm "no, they most certainly have not." The laws are, to be sure, cut off from their original historical and institutional contexts. But where Spinoza says that "the whole law of Moses was concerned with nothing but the Hebrew state, and consequently with nothing but corporeal advantages," and that for but a limited time, Maimonides would argue in return that the utility of the commandments – their reason and purpose – goes beyond their original rationale and lies in the contribution they make, at any time, to the Jewish people's material, social, and intellectual well-being. They contribute to the perfection of those who follow them as citizens and as human beings.

Maimonides' rationalization of Jewish law was controversial in its time. Medieval rabbinic critics argued that it is wrong to seek reasons for commandments that should be accepted just because they come from God.[21] It is worth noting, however, that Maimonides' views on this are endorsed six centuries later in the writings of yet another famous Moses, namely, Moses Mendelssohn.[22] In his treatise *Jerusalem, or On Religion and Power and Judaism* (1783), Mendelssohn rejects the idea that at the core of Judaism are irrational "mysteries" or fundamental principles opaque to reason. It is true that the Law was revealed by God to Moses "in a miraculous and supernatural manner ... The Israelites possess a divine legislation – laws, commandments, ordinances, rules of life, instruction in the will of God as to how they should conduct themselves." However, the utilitarian purpose of the law is clear and accessible to human thought. "The written as well as the unwritten laws [made known by God] have directly, as prescriptions for action and rules of life, public and private felicity as their ultimate aim." The laws

---

[21] Ya'akov ben Asher (ca. 1270–1340) insisted that "We do not need to ask the reason for the commandments, for it is the king's decree that is obligatory even if we do not know the reason" (quoted in Seeman 2013: 298n2).

[22] Mendelssohn, however, is not uncritical of Maimonides. He is especially troubled by Maimonides' effort to introduce essential doctrines or "articles of faith" into Judaism; see Mendelssohn 1983: 100–101.

of Judaism, for Mendelssohn, guide us toward the knowledge of truths, foster proper social relations, and – in a kind of echo of the tension in Maimonides between the moral life and the contemplative life – "establish a connection between action and contemplation, life with theory."[23]

Judaism as a Rational Religion

Julius Gutmann famously argued that the intellectual tradition that is often called "Jewish philosophy" is better understood as philosophies *of* Judaism. By this he understood philosophy that takes Judaism as its object of study, or "those systems of thought specifically concerned with the interpretation and justification of the Jewish religion."[24] I suggest that Maimonides' account of Jewish law certainly does qualify as a philosophy of Judaism. To the extent that the Law – the *mitzvot* of Torah – constitutes the essential core of Judaism, Maimonides' rationalization of those commandments is a rationalization of Judaism itself. Judaism becomes a religion of reason. What this means is that questions regarding "Why?" – not just *first-order* questions about why worship is done in this way rather than that, or why some foods are permitted and others are not, but also *second-order* questions as to the status of those laws and why one should follow them – have answers that are meant to appeal to reason. The normative force of Jewish Law, the obligatoriness of its imperative content, derives not only from the fact that the commandments come from God but also from their reasonableness. One is not asked to do or believe this or refrain from doing or believing that out of mere faith, without rational justification. One may certainly observe the commands of the God of Judaism just because that God commands them. That is, perhaps, how Maimonides envisions the obedience to the commandments among the multitude. But according to Maimonides, there is, behind those *mitzvot*, a reasonable scheme of things, one that brings benefits both to the individuals who observe them and to the society in which they must live.

The same witnesses who testified that among the "abominable heresies" that Spinoza said earned him a *herem* was his view that "the Law is not true" report that he told them that he was punished for claiming, as

[23] Mendelssohn 1983: 90, 128.   [24] Guttmann 1964.

well, that "God exists only philosophically." Presumably this means a depersonalized God, merely an infinite and eternal cause of things that is devoid of any familiar psychological and moral characteristics and thus not a deity whom one would worship or pray to or in whom one would seek comfort – in other words, the God that appears some years later in the *Ethics* as *Deus sive Natura*, God or Nature. As we have seen, Maimonides might reasonably be accused of taking a similar theological posture, although certainly not so explicitly. His God, too, appears to be merely a "philosophical God."

Likewise, one might argue that Maimonides has so transformed Judaism that it barely looks like a religion at all.[25] It does seem as if in the *Guide* Maimonides has rationalized and demythologized Judaism to such a degree that it is emptied of any mystical or numinous aspects.[26] All that is left, a critic could complain, is a metaphysical and ethical theory rather than a religion proper. My guess is that Maimonides would throw this accusation right back at his opponent and argue that, at least for those ready to understand the truth, he has in fact purified Judaism of its superstitious and irrational elements, many of which undermine faith, and saved it from the clutches of mystics and obscurantists. That, at least, is what I believe *my* Maimonides would say.

---

[25] My thanks to Ken Seeskin for raising this issue with me.
[26] To be fair, there is the difficult doctrine of the intense, passionate love of, and "bond" with, God that is presented in the final chapters of the *Guide* (III.51–53), which I do not discuss here but which has often received a rather mystical interpretation. However, here, too, I believe that Maimonides is ultimately an arch-rationalist; see Nadler 2021.

CHAPTER 5

Why Read Maimonides Today?

When Socrates finally has the opportunity to present his defense (*apologia*) to the Athenian jury, he takes an unusual strategy. Rather than asking for forgiveness and throwing himself on the mercy of his judges – "You would have liked to hear me weep and wail," he tells them – or appealing to their emotions by having his wife and children come before the court to plead for his life, he simply describes his mission in life.

> I have never lived an ordinary, quiet life. I did not care for the things that most people care about – making money, having a comfortable home, high military or civil rank, and all the other activities, political appointments, secret societies, party organizations, which go on in our city. . . . Instead of taking a course which would have done no good either to you or to me, I set myself to do for you individually in private what I hold to be the greatest possible service. I tried to persuade each one of you not to think more of practical advantages than of his mental and moral well-being.[1]

Socrates has earned the enmity of the city's leading citizens for the way in which, over many years, he pressed and baited them, hoping to get them to see that they were not living rightly. He sought to persuade them that they should reorder their priorities and give more care to character and the condition of the soul than to such ephemeral goods as wealth and power. "Are you not ashamed," he chided them, "that you give your attention to acquiring as much money as possible, and similarly with reputation and honor, and give no attention or thought to truth and understanding and the perfection of your soul?"[2] Above all, he urged them, consider not only the things you pursue and projects you

[1] Plato, *Apology*, 36b–c.   [2] Plato, *Apology*, 29d–e.

undertake in light of your beliefs and values but, more importantly, the beliefs and values themselves that inform your life. What really matters to you? Are you truly virtuous and, consequently, truly flourishing?

These, Socrates believed, are the most important questions of all. Although the object of investigation – oneself – is close at hand, the task is exceedingly difficult. However, the person who fails even to engage in critical self-examination and ask such questions cannot begin to live a truly good human life. As Socrates proclaims, in one of the most famous and eloquent sayings in the history of philosophy, "the unexamined life is not worth living for a human being."[3]

What Socrates means by an *examined* life is just the engagement of philosophy itself. The philosopher's vocation is to investigate things – to study the world, to be sure, but especially to study herself and others: how we live and, more important, how we ought to live. What she will thereby discover through philosophy, in a neat circle, is that the best way to live is to philosophize. Toward the end of his trial, Socrates considers the possibility that he might be acquitted but only on one condition. As he imagines the jurors framing the offer, they propose "that you give up spending your time on this quest and stop philosophizing." He says he would, of course, reject any such deal. "So long as I draw breath and have my faculties, I shall never stop practicing philosophy and exhorting you and elucidating the truth for everyone that I meet."[4] Philosophy for Socrates is not just a matter of armchair reflection on this or that problem or challenging thought experiments. Philosophy is a practice, a way of life. If Socrates cannot philosophize, he cannot live.

The first-century Stoic philosopher Epictetus likewise believed that living philosophically was the key to human excellence and well-being. In a period of political instability within the Greek territories of the Roman Empire, and having himself once been enslaved, he sought a remedy for the changes of fortune and attendant mental turmoil – the emotional ups and downs – that typically characterize human existence. We rejoice when we obtain the objects of our desires and are disturbed when we lose them. We love, we hate, we envy, we regret – all of these passionate states of mind are directed at things we value, but

---

[3] Plato, *Apology*, 38a.   [4] Plato, *Apology*, 29c–d.

things whose comings and goings are not at all under our command. We cannot fully determine whether a loved one thrives or perishes or whether we enjoy the honor of our peers or their loathing. The key to happiness, then, is simple: direct your care away from things you cannot control and focus only on those things that are truly within your power. And what is truly within your power are your states of mind – that is, the evaluations and judgments about things that give rise to the desires for them.

> Men are disturbed not by things, but by the views which they take of things. For instance, death is nothing dreadful, or else Socrates would have thought it so. No, the only dreadful thing about it is the judgment that it is dreadful. And so when we are hindered, or disturbed, or distressed, let us never lay the blame on others, but on ourselves, that is, on our own judgements.[5]

This realignment of one's concerns, away from the external world and toward what is properly "one's own," is the key to true happiness. When we no longer overly care for, chase after, or are anxious about things not within our power, there comes a calming of the passions, peace of mind, and tranquility, even a kind of freedom. The proper guide for reaching this condition of self-control and the consequent psychological and moral equanimity in the face of fortune is philosophy. For the Stoic, philosophy teaches us how to get by and even thrive in a world that is indifferent to our happiness.

> If you ever happen to turn your attention to externals, for the pleasure of anyone, be assured that you have ruined your scheme of life. Be content, then, in everything with being a philosopher; and if you wish to seem so likewise to anyone, appear so to yourself, and it will suffice you. ... You must be one person, either good or bad. You must cultivate either your own reason or externals; apply yourself either to things within or without you—that is, be either a philosopher or one of the mob.[6]

It is the philosopher who knows how to live, and who lives as he knows.

We find practically the same lessons, and the same tribute to the philosophical life, centuries later in Spinoza's philosophy. In his masterpiece, the *Ethics*, Spinoza demonstrates how our lives are ordinarily lived

---

[5] Epictetus, *Enchiridion*, V. [6] Epictetus, *Enchiridion*, XXIII, XXIX.

in "bondage" to the passions, to the ways in which we suffer affective changes brought about by things outside us. All of our desires and actions are directed toward the individuals or objects we love because they makes us feel good, while we strive to avoid those people or things we hate because they cause sadness or pain. It is a life in thrall especially to the irrational feelings of hope and fear, which are fixated (with great emotional disquiet) on what may or may not come our way.

Like the Stoics, Spinoza is eager to show us how pathetic such a life is. When a person is chasing after ephemeral goods and therefore living at the mercy of external forces, true well-being (of which such a person has no adequate or clear and distinct conception) is outside his control. Having categorized and analyzed the emotions that govern us – especially joy and sadness and the multifarious forms they take – Spinoza concludes that "from what has been said it is clear that we are driven about in many ways by external causes, and that, like waves on the sea, driven by contrary winds, we toss about, not knowing our outcome and fate."[7]

Fortunately, there is way out of this condition. Through a kind of intellectual therapy, one can arrive at a condition of virtue, freedom (understood as personal autonomy), and happiness. We can have a life guided not by passion but by reason. In rational living, what we do is directed not by how things happen to make us feel at the moment, nor by what we, on the basis of deficient knowledge, anticipate feeling in the future, but by what we know with certainty is truly in our own best, long-term interest. The therapeutic procedure requires careful reflection on, and correction of, what one thinks one knows, leading to a better, truer understanding of the order of nature and of one's own relationship to the world. Through recalibrating one's ideas so that they are arranged not according to how they happen to arrive in the mind in random ways through sense experience and the imagination but according to the intellect so as to form a coherent, "adequate" body of knowledge, one will experience a weakening of the disruptive passions and a more informed and reliable pursuit of what is good. "The more the mind understands things," he notes, "the less it is acted upon by affects which

---

[7] Spinoza, *Ethics*, Part III, proposition 39, scholium.

are evil, and the less it fears death."[8] The payoff of the epistemic therapy and the understanding it brings are a real and lasting joy, a deep satisfaction with oneself and one's power.

> We shall bear calmly those things which happen to us contrary to what the principle of our advantage demands, if we are conscious that we have done our duty, that the power we have could not have extended itself to the point where we could have avoided those things, and that we are part of the whole of nature, whose order we follow. If we understand this clearly and distinctly, that part of us which is defined by understanding, i.e., the better part of us, will be entirely satisfied with this, and will strive to persevere in that satisfaction.[9]

What Spinoza is recommending as the path to *eudaimonia* – he also calls it "blessedness" and "salvation" – is not a one-time exercise. Rather, it is a lifelong practice, one that is both intellectual and affective. It is a matter of knowing how to live, but also – and here we have another echo of Socrates – knowing how to die, how to face mortality. It is, in fact, the practice of philosophy itself. Wisdom is both the means and the end.

> The wise man, insofar as he is considered as such, is hardly troubled in spirit, but being, by a certain eternal necessity, conscious of himself, and of God, and of things, he never ceases to be, but always possesses true peace of mind.[10]

Philosophy as a Way of Life

Socrates, Epictetus, and Spinoza are but three prominent examples of thinkers devoted to a certain conception of philosophy. For them, philosophy is not just a hobby or a pastime, something one undertakes at leisure or in one's spare time. But neither is it a professional discipline practiced only by trained and certified experts in an institutional setting. And it certainly is not found only in books. To use a phrase coined by Pierre Hadot, the French scholar of ancient thought, philosophy for them, as for many others, is "a way of life."

---

[8] Spinoza, *Ethics*, Part V, proposition 38. [9] Spinoza, *Ethics*, Part IV, Appendix, XXXII.
[10] Spinoza, *Ethics*, Part V, proposition 40.

Hadot was concerned with spiritual exercises generally – including mystical traditions and ascetic practices – and so something broader than what we today might consider "philosophy." But what he found in all of the phenomena that he studied is that they purport to offer a path to wisdom, *sophia*. For the ancients, Hadot claims,

> Philosophy took on the form of an exercise of thought, will and the totality of one's being, the goal of which was to achieve a state practically inaccessible to mankind: wisdom. Philosophy was a method of spiritual progress which demanded a radical conversion and transformation of the individual's way of being. Thus, philosophy was a way of life, both in its exercise and effort to achieve wisdom, and in its goal, wisdom itself. For real wisdom does not merely cause us to know: it makes us "be" in a different way.[11]

Hadot's understanding of philosophy as a way of life – its methods and its goals – fits well what Socrates, Epictetus, and Spinoza (despite their many important differences) believed they were up to and what they were recommending to others. "Wisdom was a way of life which brought peace of mind (*ataraxia*), inner freedom (*autarkeia*), and a cosmic consciousness." By this latter term, Hadot means a broadening of one's perception to take in the grand scheme of things and see how one fits within it – a more universal apprehension that comes through the use of reason rather than sense experience, which is highly perspectival, fleeting, and limited to particulars. "First and foremost, philosophy presented itself as a therapeutic, intended to cure mankind's anguish."[12]

Philosophy, in other words, is a form of self-transformation. In practicing *philosophia*, the love of wisdom, the means and the end are essentially one and the same. More than an epistemic training, it is an indefinitely extended existential project. To philosophize is not just to think well but to live well.

What I hope to have made clear in these chapters is that Maimonides rightly belongs with Socrates and others among those thinkers for whom philosophy is a transformative way of life, a mode of being devoted to the search for wisdom. A true polymath of legal, medical, scientific, and philosophical learning and the spiritual leader of a widely

[11] Hadot 1995: 265.   [12] Hadot 1995: 265–6.

dispersed religious community, Maimonides was concerned above all with the improvement of the self, through both study and practice, and the achievement of human flourishing. This commitment to philosophy as a means of personal and social *eudaimonia* comes out, I have proposed, in his lessons on how to read the Bible, his approach to the problem of evil, and his understanding of Judaism itself.

Better Living through Scripture . . .

The philosophically informed reader of the Bible knows how to distill truth from its passages and access the wisdom that its authors sought to convey, albeit sometimes in covert and parabolic ways. For a person of religious faith, that wisdom may be grasped as a knowledge of God and an understanding of God's ways. But the truths that Maimonides finds in the Bible (and, presumably, other prophetic writings) are supposed to enlighten us, faithful or otherwise, about the universe – the Aristotelian cosmology will have to be abandoned, but there is still much to be gleaned of a metaphysical and even a physical nature – and, he would say, especially about ourselves. Taken together, the legal and narrative elements of *TaNaKh*, when properly interpreted according to reason, direct us on how to live well with each other and how to achieve the best condition of a human being. The Law (the commandments of Torah), especially, is tailored for our personal improvement in body and mind and our social and political welfare.

It turns out, moreover, that what Maimonides thereby provides is an answer not only to the question of *how* to read the Bible but also, as I suggest in Chapter 2, to the perhaps more fundamental question of *why* read the Bible. On this, Maimonides, the twelfth-century rabbi, and Spinoza, the seventeenth-century heretic, may seem not so far apart. They agree that reading the Bible is good for us, that it can improve us and move us toward a better personal and social condition. It is a superb guide for developing virtuous character and cultivating the right way of living with others.

According to Spinoza, the best and surest way of arriving at virtue, freedom, and blessedness is through philosophy. A more perfected mind and genuinely (rationally) benevolent actions follow from an epistemic achievement that consists in a true knowledge of the essences of things and how they relate to the essence of God or Nature. This includes a philosophical/scientific understanding of the world and of oneself as a part of Nature, which in turn leads to an adequate perception of how it is genuinely in one's own best interest to improve the lives of others. Virtue for "the free person [*homo liber*]" – the ideal "model of human nature" – is a matter not of simple "obedience" to commandments supposedly issued by an anthropomorphic God (which the rationally virtuous person knows is a superstitious fiction) but of living according to the "dictates of reason."

There is not much here with which Maimonides would disagree, at least in its general rationalist features. And to the extent that a work like Maimonides' *Guide* or Spinoza's *Ethics* expounds a purely philosophical way toward a better and more virtuous life, one that is solidly grounded in knowledge and not the passions, it is in principle more effective than the Bible in leading a prepared reader to cultivate personal virtue and live ethically with others. However, both the *Guide*, with its explicitly implanted "contradictions" and concealed truths, and the *Ethics*, with its forbidding array of definitions, axioms, and propositions presented and demonstrated in a Euclidean geometric manner, are directed at a very select audience. They are extremely difficult works, practically impenetrable to the layperson. As Spinoza says in the very last words of the *Ethics*, "all things excellent are as difficult as they are rare." The philosophical path to virtue – to freedom and peace of mind and to justice, charity, and loving-kindness – is not for everyone.

Spinoza, for his part, grants that for the multitude there is a work of literature that offers a more accessible way to a better life. As we have seen, what for Spinoza makes the Bible "sacred" and "divine" is not that it derives from some transcendent, supernatural source but that it is a particularly effective work of human literature for conveying the "word of God" (treat your fellow human beings with loving-kindness) and for morally edifying and inspiring its readers. Its storytelling appeals more to the imagination than to reason, and so it does not demand sophisticated philosophical reasoning for its message to take hold.

And yet, Spinoza insists, while Scripture is admittedly well crafted for achieving this goal, it is ultimately up to the reader of the text to make it work and to elevate it to "divine" status. Spinoza reminds us that no matter how fit a book is, by its intrinsic features, for inspiring justice and charity, it can always be misused – for example, by unscrupulous ecclesiastic authorities seeking to apply the Bible's portrayal of God to manipulate the hopes and fears of ordinary people in order to gain power and influence over them. Just as a corkscrew can be employed for nefarious purposes, as a weapon, so can the Bible be abused. This is precisely Spinoza's great fear and concern in the *Theological-Political Treatise*, and why he says explicitly that the Bible "will be sacred only so long as men use it in a religious manner."[13] He has seen the way the more conservative leaders of the Dutch Reformed Church in the seventeenth century typically exploit the Bible for their own religious and political ends, encouraging in their flocks not so much justice and charity as fear and prejudice.

Thus, even though Spinoza agrees that there is no work of literature better suited for inspiring the masses to obey the word of God and practice justice and charity than the collected writings of the biblical prophets, he maintains that the divinity of Scripture is *not* an intrinsic feature of the written text, not something that is a function solely of its objective character – its narrative content and its literary style. Rather, divinity must be primarily a relative, even subjective affair. It all depends on the reader's response. Spinoza notes that "nothing is sacred or profane or impure in itself, outside the mind, but only in relation to the mind."[14] A text may be perfectly composed for its moral purpose; it may clearly and imaginatively proclaim the word of God, but if it fails actually to have the proper edifying effect on its readers, then it is not divine. On the other hand, any work of literature that does effectively arouse readers to obedience to the divine (moral) message, regardless of who the author is or what her sources are, is, for that reason alone, divine.[15]

Here we come upon another crucial and irreconcilable difference between Maimonides and Spinoza on Scripture. Maimonides could not possibly countenance such a deflationary conception of the Hebrew Bible's divinity. While his anti-anthropomorphic theology will not allow for a God who literally composes a text (either directly or by

---

[13] *Theological-Political Treatise*, XII; Spinoza 2016: 250.
[14] *Theological-Political Treatise*, XII; Spinoza 2016: 250.
[15] On this topic, see Nadler (forthcoming).

dictating to a human amanuensis), the Bible's sacredness cannot be reduced merely to the fact that it efficaciously encourages just and merciful behavior and love of our fellow human beings. For Maimonides, the divinity and sacredness of the prophetic writings is an absolute feature of the work itself, independent of how it is used and regardless of its success or failure in actually having the appropriate psychological and ethical effect on readers. It is all a matter of the prophet's own nature and his ultimate source, the divine overflow. This guarantees that his text will be special, that it will be of superlative imaginative craft and necessarily informed by the truth. The Bible for Maimonides has a unique status and does something that nonprophetic texts cannot possibly do. That is why, in his view, we should read it.

... and through Philosophy

Maimonides' approach to the theological problem of evil also represents an account of how to improve ourselves, in this case in such a way that we can reduce the role that (moral) luck plays as we navigate our way through the world and the obstacles it poses to our flourishing. Again, the key is living philosophically, that is, *doing* philosophy and thereby arriving at a better understanding of things. The more knowledge one acquires – in Maimonidean terms, the closer one comes to a "perfected intellect" – the more one enjoys protection against the vicissitudes of nature, including the harms that others may attempt to perpetrate. The philosopher, the wise person, achieves, if not a total immunity to luck, greater control over his well-being. For Maimonides, a good person is one whose beliefs, desires and engagements are all under the guidance of reason; he is in constant critical reflection upon his actions and upon the values that inform those actions. This is the path to virtue, understood both in terms of moral character, whereby one knows and follows the right way to act, and as an intellectual condition. A life of philosophizing *is* the virtuous life, and the person who chooses to perfect herself through the love and pursuit of wisdom will enjoy great benefits in this world.

Finally, there is the question of what religion is and what it can be. Maimonides points the way to a faith that is free of superstition, prejudice, and hatred. His philosophical religion – like his approach to reading the Bible and to the problem of evil and moral luck – while not without an affective dimension, is centered on reason and the intellect.[16] Judaism is, of course, his main concern, and he is absolutely focused on preserving its distinctiveness. Maimonides is not interested in fomenting a single world religion or universal faith, and (unlike Spinoza) even less in seeing Jewish law wither away. Nonetheless, the lessons he offers are – to use a term from the world of business – universally scalable. Religious differences do not have to divide us. Rather, our beliefs about God (if we have any), the cosmos, ethics and what really matters should direct us, perhaps in different and irreducible ways, toward a common good, peaceful coexistence and mutual benevolence. On this view, the notion of wars of religion should be an oxymoron.

Reading Maimonides Today

Among the traditional responsibilities of philosophers is to provide lessons on how to think well and live rightly. If there is such a thing as "true wisdom," an objective understanding of things (including human nature) that is accessible to all and that will transform our lives and brings us benefits of mind, body and action, it surely transcends historical period and geographical borders, as well as the boundaries of religious, ethnic or cultural identity. Why, then, should we not turn to a philosophically gifted rabbi living in Egypt in the twelfth century writing in Arabic and Hebrew to see what we might learn?

What I hope to have shown in this book is that Maimonides is still someone worth reading for just this reason. No less than Socrates or the ancient Stoics, and much more so than the many self-help books now available in bookstores, Maimonides is occupied with the most important questions that concern us as we seek happiness and well-being in a world in which we must both contend with forces beyond our control and live with others. What his writings offer us – Jew or gentile; religiously faithful, agnostic, or atheist – is a guide not only to the resolution of perplexity but to life – to a life of wisdom, a *good* life.

---

[16] On the topic of philosphical religion, see Fraenkel 2014.

References

Altmann, Alexander. 1972. "Maimonides' Four Perfections", *Israel Oriental Studies* 2: 15–24.
Augustine. 1989. *Saint Augustine: Letters, Volume VI (1*–29*)*, Robert B. Eno, trans. Fathers of the Church 81. Washington, DC: Catholic University of America Press.
ben Joseph, Saadya. 1948. *The Book of Beliefs and Opinions*. Samuel Rosenblatt, trans. New Haven: Yale University Press.
ben Joseph, Saadya. 1988. "The Book of Theodicy". In *Translation and Commentary on the Book of Job, by Saadiah Ben Joseph Al-Fayyumi*. Lenn Goodman, trans. New Haven: Yale University Press, 121–413.
ben Rambam, Avraham. 1953. *Sefer Milhamot ha-Shem*, ed. Reuven Margalioth. Jerusalem: Mossad Ha-Rav Kook.
Blumenthal, David. 1981. "Maimonides' Intellectualist Mysticism and the Superiority of the Prophecy of Moses", *Studies in Medieval Culture* 10: 51–77.
Davidson, Herbert. 2005. *Moses Maimonides: The Man and His Works*. Oxford: Oxford University Press.
Diesendruck, Zvi. 1936. "Samuel and Moses ibn Tibbon on Maimonides' Theory of Divine Providence", *Hebrew Union College Annual* 11: 341–66.
Eisen, Robert. 2004. *The Book of Job in Medieval Jewish Philosophy*. Oxford: Oxford University Press.
Feldman, Seymour. 2008. "Divine Omnipotence, Omniscience and Free Will." In Steven Nadler and Tamar Rudavsky, eds., *The Cambridge History of Jewish Philosophy: From Antiquity through the Seventeenth Century*. Cambridge: Cambridge University Press, 659–704.
Fraenkel, Carlos. 2014. *Philosophical Religions from Plato to Spinoza: Reason, Religion and Autonomy*. Cambridge: Cambridge University Press.
Galston, Miriam. 1978. "The Purpose of the Law according to Maimonides", *The Jewish Quarterly Review* 69: 27–51.

Gellman, Jerome. 1989. "Freedom and Determinism in Maimonides' Philosophy." In Eric Ormsby, ed., *Moses Maimonides and His Time*. Washington, DC: Catholic University Press, 139–50.

Guttmann, Julius. 1964. *Philosophies of Judaism: The History of Jewish Philosophy from Biblical Times to Franz Rosenzweig*. New York: Holt, Rinehart and Winston.

Hadot, Pierre. 1995. *Philosophy as a Way of Life*. Oxford: Blackwell.

Halbertal, Moshe. 2014. *Maimonides: Life and Thought*. Princeton: Princeton University Press.

Hartman, David. 1976. *Maimonides: Torah and Philosophic Quest*. Philadelphia: Jewish Publication Society.

Ivry, Alfred. 2005. *Maimonides' Guide of the Perplexed: A Philosophical Guide*. Chicago: University of Chicago Press.

Kellner, Menachem. 1990. *Maimonides on Human Perfection*. Atlanta: Scholars Press.

Kellner, Menachem. 2004. *Dogma in Medieval Jewish Thought: From Maimonides to Abravanel*. The Littman Library of Jewish Civilization. Liverpool: University of Liverpool Press.

Kraemer, Joel. 2008. *Maimonides: The Life and World of One of Civilization's Greatest Minds*. New York: Doubleday.

Kreisel, Howard. 1989. "Intellectual Perfection and the Role of the Law in Maimonides." In Jacob Neusner, Ernest Frerichs and Nahum M. Sarna, eds., *From Ancient Israel to Modern Judaism: Intellect in Quest of Understanding*. Atlanta: Scholars Press, 25–46.

Lasker, Daniel. 2010. "Love of God and Knowledge of God in Maimonides' Philosophy." In Jacqueline Hamesse and Olga Weijers, eds., *Écriture et réécriture des textes philosophiques médiévaux: Volume d'hommage offert à Colette Sirat*. Turnhout: Brepols, 329–45.

Leaman, Oliver. 1995. *Evil and Suffering in Jewish Philosophy*. Cambridge: Cambridge University Press.

Leibniz, Gottfried Wilhelm. 1976. *Philosophical Papers and Letters*. Dordrecht: Reidel.

Maimonides. 1963. *Guide of the Perplexed*. 2 vols. Shlomo Pines, trans. University of Chicago Press.

Maimonides. 1972. *A Maimonides Reader*. Isidor Twersky, ed. Millburn: Behrman House.

Manekin, Charles. 2005. *On Maimonides*. Belmont: Wadsworth.

Mendelssohn, Moses. 1983. *Jerusalem, or on Religious Power and Judaism*. Allan Arkush, trans. Hanover, NH: Brandeis University Press.

Nadler, Steven. 2014. *Spinoza and Medieval Jewish Philosophy*. Cambridge: Cambridge University Press.

Nadler, Steven. 2018. *Spinoza: A Life*. 2nd ed. Cambridge: Cambridge University Press.
Nadler, Steven. 2019. "The Guide of the Perplexed in Early Modern Philosophy and Spinoza." In Josef Stern, James T. Robinson and Yonatan Shemesh, eds., *Maimonides' Guide of the Perplexed in Translation: A History from the Thirteenth Century to the Twentieth*. Chicago: University of Chicago Press, 365–84.
Nadler, Steven. 2021. "Maimonides on Human Perfection and the Love of God." In Daniel Frank and Aaron Segal, eds., *The Cambridge Critical Guide to Maimonides Guide of the Perplexed*. Cambridge: Cambridge University Press, 266–85.
Nadler, Steven. Forthcoming. "Spinoza on the Divinity of Scripture." In Michael Rosenthal, ed., *Spinoza and Modern Jewish Philosophy*. New York: Palgrave MacMillan.
Nagel, Thomas. 1974. "What Is It Like To Be a Bat?" *The Philosophical Review* 83: 450.
Nagel, Thomas. 1979. "Moral Luck." In Thomas Nagel, ed., *Mortal Questions*. New York: Cambridge University Press, 34–8.
Nehorai, Michael. 1988. "Maimonides and Gersonides: Two Approaches to the Nature of Providence", *Da'at* 20: 51–64 [Hebrew].
Nemoy, Leon. 1932. *Karaite Anthology: Excerpts from the Early Literature*. New Haven: Yale University Press.
Nuriel, Avraham. 1980. "Providence and Governance in *The Guide of the Perplexed*", *Tarbiz* 49: 346–55 [Hebrew].
Nussbaum, Martha. 1986. *The Fragility of Goodness*. Cambridge: Cambridge University Press.
Pines, Shlomo. 1960. "Notes on Maimonides' Views Concerning Free Will", *Studies in Philosophy, Scripta Hierosolymitana* 6: 195–8.
Pines, Shlomo. 1979. "The Limitations of Human Knowledge According to Al-Farabi, ibn Bajja, and Maimonides." In Isidore Twersky, ed., *Studies in Medieval Jewish History and Literature*. Cambridge, MA: Harvard University Press, 1–82.
Raffel, Charles M. 1987. "Providence as Consequent upon the Intellect: Maimonides' Theory of Providence", *Association for Jewish Studies Review* 12: 25–72.
Reines, Alvin. 1972. "Maimonides' Concepts of Providence and Theodicy", *Hebrew Union College Annual* 43: 169–205.
Rudavsky, Tamar. 2010. *Maimonides*. Malden: Wiley-Blackwell.
Seeman, Don. 2013. "Reasons for the Commandments as Contemplative Practice in Maimonides", *The Jewish Quarterly Review* 103: 298–327.
Seeskin, Kenneth. 1996. *Maimonides: Guide for Today's Perplexed*. Millburn: Behrman House.

Sirat, Colette. 1985. *A History of Jewish Philosophy in the Middle Ages*. Cambridge: Cambridge University Press.
Sokol, Moshe. 1998. "Maimonides on Freedom of the Will and Moral Responsibility", *Harvard Theological Review* 91: 25–39.
Spinoza, Benedictus. 2016. *The Collected Works of Spinoza*, vol. 2. Edwin Curley, trans. and ed. Princeton: Princeton University Press.
Stern, Josef. 1986. "The Idea of a *Hoq* in Maimonides' Explanation of the Law." In Shlomo Pines and Yirmiyahu Yovel, eds., *Maimonides and Philosophy*. Archives Internationales d'Histoire des Idées/International Archives of the History of Ideas, vol. 114. Springer: Dordrecht, 92–130.
Stern, Josef. 2013. *The Matter and Form of Maimonides' Guide*. Cambridge, MA: Harvard University Press.
Stitskin, Leon D. 1973. "Maimonides' Letter on Apostasy: The Advent of the Messiah and Shivat Zion (Return to Zion)", *Tradition: A Journal of Orthodox Jewish Thought* 14: 103–12.
Stroumsa, Sarah. 2009. *Maimonides in His World: Portrait of a Mediterranean Thinker*. Princeton: Princeton University Press.
Touati, Charles. 1990a. "Les deux théories de Maïmonide sur la providence." In Charles Touati, ed., *Prophètes, Talmudistes, Philosophes*. Paris: Les Editions du Cerf.
Weiss, Raymond. 1991. *Maimonides' Ethics: The Encounter of Philosophic and Religious Morality*. Chicago: University of Chicago Press.
Whitehead, Alfred North. 1979. *Process and Reality*. New York: Free Press.
Williams, Bernard. 1976. "Moral Luck", *Proceedings of the Aristotelian Society*, Supplementary Volume L: 115–35.
Wolf, Susan. 1982. "Moral Saints", *Journal of Philosophy* 79: 419–39.

Index

Aeschylus, 9, 85
Albert the Great, 4
Alexander of Aphrodisias, 15
al-Farabi, Abu Nasr Muhammad, 15
al-Ghazali, Abu Hamid Muhammad, 15
al-Kirkisani, Jacob, 38
Almohads, 11–12
Almoravids, 11
al-Qadi al-Fadil, 14
Andalusia, 11
Aquinas, Thomas, 4, 90, 91
Aristotle, 4, 5, 9, 15, 18, 35, 43, 59–62, 63, 65, 66, 70, 75, 85, 107, 108
Asharites, 15, 75
Augustine, Bishop of Hippo, 21–2
Averroës, 15
Avicenna, 15
Ayyubids, 14

Bible
   as divine, 128–9
   how to read, 8, 23–48

Córdoba, 11

David ben Maimon, 20–1
Descartes, René, 5, 43
divine providence. *See* God, providence of

Epictetus, 43, 121–2, 124, 125
Epicureans, 4, 5, 75
Euripides, 85
evil
   nature of, 54–5
   problem of, 9, 50–4, 83–4, 129

Fatimids, 14
Fez, 11–12
freedom, 109–15
Fustat, 12–13

Gersonides, 43, 112
God
   anthropomorphizing of, 19, 27–30, 54, 74
   as lawgiver, 104–5
   incorporeality of, 23–5, 27–8, 36–7
   knowledge of, 30–4, 71
   omniscience of, 111–13
   providence of, 19, 74–82, 129
Guttmann, Julius, 74, 118

Hadot, Pierre, 124–5
Halevi, Judah, 15
Hobbes, Thomas, 43
human perfection, 68–74, 82, 99–100

Japheth ben Ali ha-Levi, 38
Jewish law, 91–109
   reasonableness of, 91–105
   transgression of, 105–9
Job, 50, 81
Joseph ben Judah, 16, 18, 62
Judaism, 6, 9
   as a rational religion, 118–19
   thirteen articles of, 13

Kalam, 18
Kant, Immanuel, 74, 86
Karaites, 38

Leibniz, Gottfried Wilhelm, 4, 5, 50, 51, 57, 58, 132

Index

Leone Ebreo, 43

Malebranche, Nicolas, 4
Manicheanism, 54
mean, doctrine of, 60–1, 63–8, 69–70, 101–2
Meister Eckart, 4
Mendelssohn, Moses, 117–18
moral luck, 8–9, 84–6
motivation, 87
Mutakallimun, 15
Mutazilites, 15

Newton, Isaac, 4

perplexity, 6, 8, 16–19
Plato, 2, 4, 5, 9, 15, 18, 71, 73, 81, 85, 88, 91
prophecy, 41–2, 105

rationalism, 5–6, 38–40, 53–4
    of Jewish law, 91–105

Saadya ben Joseph, 15, 39–40, 93–7, 99, 103
Saladin, 14, 20
Samuel ibn Tibbon, 43, 78
Socrates, 4, 55, 81, 88–9, 92, 104, 120–1, 122, 124, 125, 130
Sophocles, 9, 85
Spinoza, Bento (Baruch) de, 5, 42–8, 71, 75, 115–17, 122–4, 125, 128–9
Stoics, 4, 5, 43, 81, 85, 123, 130

theodicy, 51–4, 55–9
Toah commandments. *See* Jewish law

Umayyads, 11

virtue, 59–62, 63–8, 72–4, 100, 101–2

Whitehead, Alfred North, 2
wisdom, 62, 67–8, 70–1, 124, 125

For EU product safety concerns, contact us at Calle de José Abascal, 56–1°, 28003 Madrid, Spain or eugpsr@cambridge.org.

www.ingramcontent.com/pod-product-compliance
Lightning Source LLC
LaVergne TN
LVHW011839060526
838200LV00054B/4097